"My Cattle Look Thin"

A STORY OF
Life on a Farm in Zimbabwe

George

Best wishes,

"My Cattle Look Thin"

▲▲▲

A STORY OF

Life on a Farm in Zimbabwe

DAVID WILDING-DAVIES

Rainforest

EDITIONS

For my children,
Max, Olivia & Kate

1

A warm tropical downpour was beating on the windshield. The wipers were unable to keep up and the road ahead swam in my vision. I slowed the truck down to a crawl. My wife Amy sat next to me. The rain loudly drumming on the roof made conversation impossible. We were happier in our silence anyway, both of us quietly dealing with the emotions the trip was bringing us. In the back seat were our two children. Max, our eldest, was now a young teenager. He remembered enough and shared the apprehension of the adults in the front seat. Next to him sat Olivia. Being younger, her memories were fainter and of mostly happy times.

As suddenly as it started, the rain stopped. Instead of taking the humidity out of the air, it had increased it and warm fog hung over the countryside. Our vehicle began to pick up pace, but still our progress was slow. The road, which had five years earlier been a well-maintained tar road, now resembled a dry riverbed. The paved section had always been narrow, allowing room for only one vehicle. If you encountered an oncoming vehicle, both vehicles would have to move onto the shoulder to pass. Now the pavement had eroded in from the edges so much that it was hard to keep both wheels on it. The shoulder had washed away, so there was a sizeable drop from the pavement to shoulder. Where the pavement was most narrow, one side of the truck would suddenly drop as a wheel went off the road.

There was no sign of people anywhere. They had fled years ago. Some to escape the beatings, rapes and political indoctrination. Some to escape the hunger and hopelessness of a failed economy.

"Surely there must be someone left here," I said to Amy.

Amy looked sad and muttered, "How could one man's love for power destroy so many lives? Who in their right mind could live under such a repressive regime?"

But then, we saw a lone figure. He was in what had once been a manicured tea garden. The tea had been abandoned and had grown into a small forest. The man was wielding a machete and was cutting the tea plants to make poles for building a hut.

I remembered in the past when we would drive this road, people would be everywhere – going to work, going to school, going shopping. Most would wave at us, a few would glare. Often an open hand wave would flash at us in a show of political solidarity. Sometimes when you waved back, the open hand would be curled into a fist of the political party that wanted to destroy us.

I was questioning whether this trip was a good idea. Maybe it is better to forget and get on with one's life. Was I going to again feel the anger and rage that was necessary to live in an environment of constant danger? Was I going to feel the need for retribution or would I remember all the happy times? I knew Amy was thinking the same. Neither of us talked a lot about our emotions, but in our quiet way we each knew what the other was feeling. As I thought about it, I realized what I really felt was just sadness and a sense of loss.

The fog was lifting, revealing more of the countryside to us. The tires would rumble as we drove over the cattle grids that marked the boundaries of what had once been farms. As we passed each farm, I asked the children if they remembered the farm and the family who had lived there. Everyone remembered Denis's farm and the beautiful lodge he built in the rainforest. As we drove past what had been Big Pete's farm, Max chuckled and reminded us of the time I had shot out Big Pete's dining room window.

We were approaching our destination – what had been Ashanti Coffee Estate. We slowed down. There was no coffee in the fields, only weeds. Nature was reclaiming the land at a rate that only happens in the tropics. We stopped at the laneway that led to the homestead. We parked and I got out. I looked for signs of tire tracks in the dirt. I found none. Although we could not see the homestead that was tucked over a little hill at the end of the laneway, I felt sure it was deserted.

Olivia asked what had happened to her ponies and pets, but Max interrupted, "Why don't we move right back in and get farming again, Dad."

"We could move right back in, Max, but it would only last a short while and we would be driven out. There is no way the political powers would allow us to stay."

I didn't want to see anymore. I turned the truck around and we drove back the way we came. It was hard to believe that fifteen years ago things had been so different. We had been filled with nervous excitement as we waited to move to what was to be our new home in a country we had fallen in love with.

The devastating cyclone of 2000 had blown in from Mozambique, bringing heavy rain and wind along the border with Zimbabwe. The cyclone washed out bridges and sections of the road leading to the coffee and tea growing district of Zimbabwe known as the Eastern Highlands. Amy, Max, then three years old, Olivia, just one year old, and myself were waiting in the capital, Harare, to move to our new farm.

It is normally a six hour drive, four hours east to Mutare, the provincial capital of Manicaland, and then two hours south. The last hour is a climb up a winding road to an area known as Chipinge. The landscape changes from dry savannah to lush semitropical countryside as one travels to higher altitude. The higher rainfall creates rushing rivers that cascade down through gorges and valleys. One of these rivers, the Tanganda, had been unable to handle the rain brought by the cyclone and bursting its banks had washed out bridges and parts of the road. The town of Chipinge and the surrounding farms had been cut off from the rest of the country. After ten days of around-the-clock work, the road was again passable and people and goods could tentatively move to and from Chipinge.

We left Harare in a green pickup truck with our dog, cat and two pet geese. Our belongings followed in a moving van. With us was Rhoda who helped look after the house and the children. The driver of the moving van wanted to allow a full day to drive the last stretch of road up to Chipinge. Although the road was now open, there were still some sections that would be difficult to get through. We spent the night in Mutare with some friends and our animals stayed at the local SPCA.

We left early the next morning for the final drive. The sky was beautifully clear and as we drove south from Mutare through the communal lands the sun was rising, giving the countryside that distinctive African golden start to a new day. Children were walking to school; small, thin cattle with enormous horns were being driven to grazing lands; groups of people stood by the roadside in conversation, and women carried large bundles of firewood and containers of water on their heads.

We turned off the main road onto a smaller road at a place called Tanganda Halt and began the climb up to Chipinge.

The landscape was still typical lowveld – baobab trees with thick trunks and branches that made them look as though they were planted upside down, thorn trees, and sweetgrass growing amongst the scrub.

After climbing for a while we passed two magnificent baobabs on each side of the road, known as the gates of Chipinge. Soon the vegetation began to change. Baobabs were replaced by flat-topped acacias, magnificent mahogany trees and clumps of bamboo. We crossed a cattle grid, which marked the boundary of the communal lands and the commercial farming district.

The first commercial farm we passed was *Drie Span Berg*, meaning Three Span Mountain in Afrikaans. The name was taken from the pioneers who first trekked up to Chipinge. Their wagons had to be pulled by three span of oxen to climb this section of road. The pioneers were coming to take up Cecil John Rhode's offer of free land. Rhodes had outmaneuvered the Portuguese, who had claimed this land as part of Portuguese East Africa, through some daring and clever moves. He annexed it to the new nation that bore his name, Rhodesia. He quickly encouraged settlers to trek up from South Africa with the promise of land. In return, they were to be a buffer to the Portuguese.

We then came to the first section of road that had been washed out. A detour had been cut in the hillside beside the road. It was very rough and just wide enough for one vehicle to pass. We had to wait while a few cars came down then we drove our pickup through the detour. It was just passable for us and I had doubts that the moving van would make it. The driver walked the detour route and said he felt he could do it. He negotiated the narrow detour slowly and with a few tense moments managed to get through.

We drove through the next farm, which was Buffel's Drift. Sections of the hillside had slid onto the road and were still being cleared off by work gangs. We slowly climbed up the road. The air became cleaner and crisper as we got higher and the farms began to change from grazing lands to plantations of bananas, coffee, and wattle. The worse sections of the road were behind us now.

Five kilometres before the town of Chipinge, we turned onto

the Eastern Border Road. This road runs parallel to the border of Mozambique and some of the best coffee farms are along it. The rainfall is plentiful; the altitude is high enough to ensure a slow bean development but not so high as to risk frost. A frost will kill the coffee bushes. Twenty kilometres along this road was our destination: Ashanti Coffee Estate.

As we drew closer, we had the mixed feelings of excitement, nervousness, and apprehension about the venture we were about to embark upon. Amy and I had never farmed before, in fact until a few months earlier we had never even seen a coffee bush. We had moved to Zimbabwe from Canada two years earlier. In Canada, we had made our living with horses. We taught riding, trained and sold horses. We both had competed extensively and I had ridden on our National Three Day Event Team in the Olympics and World Championships.

We had been out to Zimbabwe on holiday and had fallen in love with the country. Maybe it was the excitement of living in a place where everything is starker and in greater contrast. Death is always closer; whether it be accidents on the motorway, disease, or wild animals. Maybe because of this, people in Africa live harder. Caution is thrown to the wind whether it be at a party, or in business, or in love. There is a lot less time for political correctness, or the need for conformity. People get on with living their lives to the fullest. There is no "nanny state" to look after you. You rely on your friends and community. The sense of community is strong and the friendships solid.

Amy and I felt Zimbabwe was a place where we could happily live. We had saved some money from our horse business and a friend was prepared to chip in some money as well. We were going to be farmers. We had always had a dream to farm and Zimbabwe struck us as the ideal place to realize these plans. Rainfall was plentiful, the climate ideal and the land was fertile and affordable. At that time, the country was heavily into agriculture and considered the breadbasket of Africa.

Every imaginable crop was grown in the country and we looked at many different types of farms. But we had our hearts set on coffee, mostly because it is grown in the most beautiful part of the country. There is nothing prettier than the neat rows of coffee planted along contour lines.

We turned off the tar road and, after driving for a kilometer along the farm road, arrived at the farm. There was big excitement among the Africans as they were all anxious to see what the new owners were like.

Rhoda, our maid from Harare, is a Ndebele from the southern part of the country. She stared at the local people, who were Ndau, with a hint of suspicion and superiority. Before the Europeans had settled the country the Ndebele had ruled over the other tribes in the region.

The founder of the Ndebele nation was Mzilikazi. He had been a lieutenant of the famous Zulu chief, Shaka, but in 1823 they quarreled and Mzilikazi rebelled. Facing execution, he fled north from South Africa with his people, conquering and absorbing other tribes. He eventually ended up in Zimbabwe, but not before being separated from the bulk of his people. They had given him up for dead and appointed his son as successor to rule over their new conquests north of the Limpopo River. When Mzilikazi was reunited with his tribe he reasserted his control by having his son and the chiefs who had appointed him killed by being thrown over a cliff. Firmly back in control of the Matebele tribe, Mzilikazi ruled over the land that is present day Zimbabwe. The numerically superior Shona tribes of Zimbabwe became the vassals of the Ndebele. The Ndebele collected tribute from the Shona and harshly punished even the most minor infractions. In 1893, Mzilikazi's son Lobengula, lost the kingdom his father created to Cecil Rhodes and the British. The Ndebele's short stabbing spear was no match for the Gatling gun. For the next 87 years the white man ruled over the people.

In 1980, Robert Mugabe, a member of the Shona tribe, was elected Prime Minister in the country's first universal suffrage election. In 1983, Mugabe used his notorious Fifth Brigade, who had been trained by the North Koreans, to launch a campaign of slaughter against the Ndebele. It was done in the most evil and cruel ways to indelibly etch fear in the minds of the Ndebele for generations to come. The Shona now ruled the people of Zimbabwe.

Rhoda however, never forgot that she was the descendent of the great Mzilikazi and, in her mind, as a member of the Ndebele people she knew she was superior to their former vassals.

Rhoda turned to me and said, "Eee boss these Ndau are very primitive and they have very strong *mushonga*."

Mushonga is witchcraft and Rhoda assured me that since she was educated she didn't believe in it, however, she said one must be careful. She remained quite aloof.

The workers seemed very cheerful and greeted us respectfully. The head foreman, in traditional African greeting, inquired about our health, the journey and welcomed us to Ashanti. He gave out a few orders and the workers jumped onto the truck and formed a chain. Everything was passed down the line and into the house. I had thought that the unloading of the moving van would take the whole afternoon, but everything was unloaded and in the house in a matter of minutes.

Russell Yeatman, Ashanti's former owner came by with his wife. They brought a hamper full of sandwiches and other foods for lunch. We all sat on the lawn and ate.

Russell had three farms in the district. They were all close to each other and he had run them as one big farm. Because of some financial difficulties, he put Ashanti up for sale. He and his family had lived on Ashanti until a few months ago when the thatch roof on the house started to leak. They now lived across the road on another of his farms.

Russell helped us by wiring in the stove and getting the hot water turned on. They took their leave and we agreed to meet first thing in the morning so he could give me a hand getting the farm started.

Our new neighbours, who lived on the farm next to us, came by and introduced themselves as Max and Sandy. They were our age and had children a little older than ours. Sandy was blonde and pretty and Max had the rugged good looks of a man used to being outside. Max had a lightning fast sense of humour and in no time had us laughing. He thought it very funny that as most white Zimbabweans were trying to leave the country, we actually wanted to come.

They had baked a cake as a house-warming gift. We took an immediate liking to them and they kindly offered to help us with advice and equipment. Our son Max who was in the middle of potty training was running around the lawn. Sandy scooped him up in her arms and gave him a big hug and spun around with him. She put him down and the front of her jersey was covered in poo! Amy and I were embarrassed, but the older Max was roaring with laughter.

Towards the end of the day, our guests left and the workers went home. We sat down at the back of the house. The homestead was built at the edge of a hill. The lawn went for six metres from the back of the house where it met a large retaining wall. The lower part of the farm could be seen from here and the view went all the way to the Mozambique border. Our house faced east and we would have the most magnificent sunrises. The house had an acre of gardens with exotic flowers and trees. There was a stable for the polocrosse ponies and a henhouse for the chickens. Just outside the yard, was a small dairy where the household cow was milked. We reflected on the venture we were setting out on.

After searching for two years, we had finally managed to buy a farm. Ashanti was run down and hadn't been properly run for some years, but it had been a nice farm. We felt it had great potential to be a lovely coffee farm again. We had never farmed before and certainly knew nothing about coffee farming, but we were about to give it a go.

Amy had followed me on this venture with good nature. In the back of my mind I hoped it wasn't a foolish decision to take up a career for which we had no previous knowledge, in a country we didn't really know. I wondered what Max meant when he said that most white Zimbabweans were trying to leave.

The farm consisted of 325 acres. We had a section along the tar road that was flat with sandy soils. The land then dropped down into a valley. These slopes had three fields that were divided by steep ravines called *gwashas*. In the gwashas were small spring fed streams and the sides of the ravines were covered in thick tropical forest. Living in the forests were monkeys and a large variety of birds; my favorite being the purple-crested lourie. The purple-crested lourie is green with a purple head and, as it flies, a bright red wing patch can be seen. We also had parrots and sunbirds. Sunbirds are nectar feeders, like humming birds, and have gorgeous iridescent plumage.

A river ran through the valley. It was called the Chinyakonya River. In the local dialect, it means the small river that mixes, a testament to the rapid flow of water over waterfalls and chutes. It rose on our northern neighbour's farm, flowed through our farm, and then on to Mozambique and the Indian Ocean. Along the river, a furrow diverted water into a dam. A pump brought water up to the top of the farm where it was held in a concrete reservoir. The water was gravity-fed to the house and coffee factory. A second pump pumped it along underground pipes in the top fields. Every so often there would be a hydrant that could be connected to an irrigation pipe to water the coffee. The fields on the slopes were fed by gravity.

On the other side of the valley there were four smaller fields. To get to them involved crossing a bridge and climbing up a steep incline. The road made a few turns through a forest and then came out into the first field. These were the smallest of our fields, but they were certainly the prettiest. The last could only be accessed by foot through a footpath that crossed a gwasha with huge mahogany trees that towered above.

We had a waterfall where we would take the children swimming. The Chinyakonya dropped six metres over a rock ledge into a sandy pool. All around the waterfall was jungle and vines hung over the pool. Even on the hottest days the air was cool and refreshing.

This was to be our home and passion. It would bring experiences we never imagined we would know. One of the early coffee farmers, who like a lot of the British left India at independence in 1948, gave the farm an Indian name, *Ashanti*. It means "excitement" or "no peace." It was to be an appropriate name. However, for us our first concern was learning how to grow coffee.

△△△
2
▽▽▽

*T*he first night sleeping in our new home, I was restless. Unlike in Harare, there was drumming coming from the farm villages until late into the night. I was so excited about the new farm that I could not fall asleep. When I did fall asleep, I kept waking up every half hour, afraid that I had slept through my alarm clock.

At five o'clock, it went off but I was fully awake. I dressed, brushed my teeth and grabbed a quick bite to eat. The sun was rising over the valley and a broad band of sunlight was moving from our house on top of the hill, through the valley and burning off the morning mist. Doves were calling and a flock of parrots screeched overhead. From the farm village came the smell of smoke from the cooking fires. Roosters were crowing, accenting the rhythmic thumping of corn being pounded into flour for the morning meals.

I headed off across the road to the farm where the former owner of Ashanti, Russell, now lived. I was to meet him at 6:00 a.m. and have him give me a hand getting started. When I arrived I went to his farm office. There was nobody around. Twenty minutes later he sauntered up. It occurred to me that he ran a very laid-back farm. A few minutes later his workers began to arrive. He introduced me to his labour force. Some of the faces I recognized from helping us unload our goods from the day before.

Some of the foremen wore faded coveralls; other workers wore clothes that were little more than rags. Their shirts were so threadbare they were on the verge of disintegrating and their trousers ended just below the knees in ripped threads. No one wore anything on his or her feet. Incredibly, some of the men wore wool toques and others the quilted hoods that had once zipped onto winter jackets. I thought of making a joke about being prepared for an unexpected tropical snowstorm but decided against it as they appeared to be quite proud of their headgear.

Russell asked the men who would like to work for me. Some of them were already living at Ashanti and said they would work for me so they could continue to stay where they were living. Others wanted to continue working for Russell and would move to one of his other farms, Excalibur or Lilesvlei.

Slowly, we put together a complete work force for Ashanti. There was a supervisor, a tractor driver, two foremen, a clerk, and twenty general labourers. Russell gave me a few pointers on how to keep records of the days worked, the rate of pay, and a brief background on some of the key people in my new work force. Then, with my new crew, I headed back across the road to Ashanti.

Russell had done very little on the farm for a number of years and really nothing the last six months. I discussed where to start with the supervisor and foremen. We decided that, since we could hardly see the coffee for all the weeds, the most appropriate starting place would be to slash the weeds that were growing in the coffee. Some of the coffee trees had vines growing up them; others had grass growing around them that was as high as the bushes. I went into town and bought fifteen scythes, called *bembas*. I returned to the farm and the crew went to work cutting the weeds. I dropped by the house to see how Amy was doing. It was now almost midday and Amy reprimanded me for not eating anything and told me to slow down. The whole thing was so exciting for me, I forgot to have breakfast.

Amy was trying to get a handle on the gardens. Russell had left a gardener named Petros to keep things in a reasonable state after he moved to his other farm. The grass had been cut and the flowerbeds weeded. Petros didn't speak a word of English and Amy didn't speak a word of Shona. He was trying to speak to Amy in *Chi-Lapalapa,* which is the language that was developed in the mines as a *lingua franca.* It uses Zulu and Shona words and the grammar is similar to English. *Lapa* means "here," "put here," "come here," etc. The words, lapa lapa, are frequent and hence the language name Chi-Lapalapa.

Amy and Petros weren't getting too far. I tried to speak to him in my limited Shona but he kept answering me in Chi-Lapalapa. It seemed that Chi-Lapalapa, a language that neither Amy nor I spoke, was going to be the only way to communicate with our gardener. We could not ask him about the flowers and trees. We could only say in Chi-Lapalapa things like: "weed here" or "plant here" or "put here." He would answer back "put well," which in Chi-Lapalapa was *fuga mushi.* Amy and I gave Petros the nickname, Fuga Mushi.

I left Amy and went back out to the fields to see how the slashing of weeds was going. I could see the gang working a distance off across the field. They looked as though they were motionless but as I approached it became apparent that they were moving and as I got closer, I could see that they were indeed working very hard. I was to learn that this is a very common optical illusion in Africa.

With the weeds cut back from around the coffee I could see the condition of the plants. It didn't look very promising.

When I had first looked at the farm three months ago, the coffee didn't look great but it was okay. The previous owner, Russell, had been having financial difficulties and the bank had cut off his credit. He hadn't fertilized for some time and was trying to grow the coffee organically. Our closing was delayed by the bank, which wanted to ensure that they had their loans repaid before releasing the title deeds.

It took a period of intense negotiation between the bank and us before everyone was satisfied and the deal completed. During this time the coffee was neglected. Looking at the coffee that was emerging from grass and vines, I was having doubts that we would get much of a crop off.

After a couple of weeks, we had enough of the weeds slashed around the coffee to start to get an idea of the condition of the plants and what we were seeing was discouraging. Amy and I had hoped to get an adequate crop off the first year and use that money to help get things going. I was unsure how to proceed. Luckily for us, we were able to get some good advice from a neighbouring farmer, Tim Fennel.

Tim was the biggest and most successful coffee farmer in the district. His family had been farming coffee for generations; first in India and after India's independence they moved to Africa and pioneered the coffee industry in Zimbabwe. Tim and his family were pillars of the community. Tim had won the coveted Coffee Grower of the Year Award almost every year, was chairman of the Coffee Growers' Association, and was one of the best polocrosse players in the world. His presence and stature were impressive and his voice deep and rich. He was renowned for his generosity. Each year, the Chipinge Polocrosse Club had a person responsible for fundraising. They would form a committee and organize fundraising events. Whenever Tim held this position he would ask his committee how much money needed to be raised? Then he took out his chequebook, wrote a cheque for that amount and declared the fundraising was over for the year and everyone could retire to the bar.

One Sunday morning, Tim drove up to our gate. He had noticed that we were bumbling along and had decided to get us on the right track. We walked together into the first coffee field. I was anxious to show Tim the farm and the work we had done so far. After five minutes, Tim turned to me and said, "David, you are stuffing around here. If you continue like this you will be out of business in two years. With coffee you have got to do things right. There are no half measures.

Every coffee tree on this farm has to be stumped out and the whole farm replanted. You will have no income for three years but if you do things right, you will pay back the farm and have money left over with your first crop."

Not exactly the words I wanted to hear but after discussing it with Amy, we agreed that Tim was right. Tim also told me to come over to his farm as he had something for me. Later that day I drove over to his farm, Dandoni. Tim and I walked down a farm track until we came upon a herd of dairy cattle grazing. Tim said, "David a farm is not complete until you have a herd of cattle. They give you and your workers milk and meat, but more importantly you can watch your herd grow, reflect on their condition, and enjoy the peace and contentment that a herd of grazing cattle exude."

He then selected two cows, both in calf, and gave them to Ashanti.

That evening Amy and I sat on our veranda looking out across our valley. As the sun set, we watched a line of darkness march up the hill on the opposite side of the valley called Excalibur. The sounds of birds going to roost gave way to the insects of the night. A baboon barked in the distance and the drumming began from the farm villages. Our two cows walked into the farmyard of their new home. Further from our valley, the lights from other farms came on and flickered in the distance and just faintly, one could hear music coming from the beer hall in the little village of Junction Gate.

Amy and I felt content. We had a plan. The farm was to be replanted. We would have to find a way to make do with no crop for three years but the end result would be worth it.

△△△

3

▽▽▽

*O*ur decision was made. Our first job was to stump out all the old coffee and burn it. The workers, now dressed in newly acquired overalls with Ashanti Coffee Estate stenciled on the back and armed with mattocks, started digging out the coffee. The uprooted plants were placed in windrows and allowed to dry, then set on fire. For weeks a blanket of smoke hung over the farm. After the first burning, remaining sticks and leaves were raked back into windrows and burnt again. We wanted to leave no old coffee vegetation that might be harbouring disease on the land.

Slowly, field-by-field, the coffee plants were taken out. The fields looked smaller without them, as if they shrunk with being fallow. Before, to cross the fields, I would have to weave my way through old coffee growing three metres high. Now, I could stride across the fields in a few short minutes.

The lands were prepared for plowing. All visible rocks were removed and lime was spread on the ground to turn in and sweeten the soil. Our one little tractor started on the seemingly insurmountable task of plowing 125 acres. In fact, it would have been insurmountable had not Tim and two other neighbours come to our aid.

I was having breakfast when I heard the big roar of diesel engines. I thought our little tractor had lost its muffler. I ran out to the fields and saw three big tractors roaring up and down the field turning over the ground at quite a pace. Somewhere in their midst, our little tractor was chugging away covered in dust. When I spoke to the drivers of the big tractors they said they had been sent by Tim and two other neighbours to plow our whole farm. I was to house them, put diesel in the tractors and they would stay until everything was done. They said the owners of the tractors wanted no payment.

After the plowing was complete, more lime was spread and disced into the ground. The fields were ready. It was time for Ashanti to be reborn as a coffee estate.

Coffee is planted at the start of the rains so the little seedlings get established before the dry season. The rains were still weeks away and the temperature was rising daily. The air was becoming full of dust as the winds blew in from the east across our bare fields. Little dust devils would twist through the farm village and the children would run giggling after them. The smell of smoke grew stronger daily, as fires raged in Mozambique. Fires that were started to clear land for planting but, carried by the wind, spread uncontrollably until at night the eastern horizon glowed orange. In our fallow fields, rain lilies magically appeared after lying dormant since the last time the fields were fallow; their pink and white flowers splashes of colour in a brown landscape.

One morning the wind stopped blowing. Later that day it returned, but now from the west. In the distance, thunder cells began to form. Danmore, our farm supervisor, came to me and said, "Boss, the rains want to come now, we must organize seedlings."

Coffee plants are started from seed in a nursery that is just a shade cloth supported by poles about two-and-a-half metres off the ground.

The shade cloth allows reduced sunlight through to the young coffee plants. Virgin soil is dug up and taken from a forested area. The soil is screened to remove any stones or sticks. Lime and fertilizer are mixed into the soil. A gang of women fills plastic pots with the soil. Each lady has a *gwaza* of pots to fill. A gwaza is a set number that the foreman has worked out to be a reasonable daily task. Once she has completed her gwaza, she goes home. The women sit on the ground and pack the soil into the pots. There is lots of chatter and gossiping. Once she has completed her gwaza she calls over a foreman who counts the filled pots. He has a stick, which he uses to make a little mark in the soil on the top of the pot so he doesn't count the same pot twice. He also checks to see that the soil is packed down in the pot. If the soil is too loose the seedling won't grow well. Any pots that are too loose are emptied out and redone before they are counted and the gwaza considered complete.

The seedlings in the nursery at Ashanti were not in the best of condition. Different varieties were mixed together and seedlings were weak. After some deliberation it was decided to buy better seedlings from other farmers. It is very important to plant strong seedlings to get a good start to the plantation. We were going to plant 150,000 coffee trees. It was a big job finding that number of sturdy seedlings.

The tea and coffee estate down the road from us had surplus seedlings. It is a big publicly owned company and runs five estates. They put in a big nursery each year. It was close to us and not difficult to move the seedlings. But, we still needed more seedlings. The best seedlings were the furthest from us, the other side of Chipinge. They were grown by a young farmer who was meticulous in his growing of coffee seedlings and it showed. Every seedling was a perfect little coffee plant. He had a big cattle truck we used to transport them and we put planks through the railings to create three different levels. It still took many trips to get all the seedling moved to Ashanti and we were under a tight time schedule.

27

The earliest time to plant coffee is August when the risk of cold weather has past. After Christmas, there is not enough of the rainy season left to get the seedlings well established before the dry season. We had five months to plant 150,000 seedlings.

Getting the whole planting process to run smoothly takes a lot of skillful workers, good logistics, and planning. Before we started planting, our foremen, most senior staff and I went next door to Tim's farm for training. Everything on Tim's farm is immaculate and his planting is no exception. We spent a week learning from his foremen about their system of planting coffee. We felt confident and went back to Ashanti to train our gangs on how we were going to plant our coffee seedlings. It proved to be much harder than expected to get everyone on the same system and planting the coffee with the consistent care. We knew that the way the coffee was planted would reflect how successful the plantation would be over the next seven years of the coffee's life.

Danmore worked tirelessly coaxing and cajoling everyone to learn. He organized competitions to see who could plant the best and remember the correct sequence of steps. He decided to have specific gangs to do each step of the planting process. Slowly we started to get it together and the planting began to pick up speed. We added more people and ended up with a total planting force of three hundred people all working together and doing an excellent job.

The planting would go like this: planting holes are measured and pegged. Our coffee was to be planted one-and-a-half metres apart in the lines and three-and-a-half metres apart in the rows. A gang using tape measures, strings, and measuring sticks, peg out where the holes should be. Another gang digs the holes with traditional African hoes called *badzas*. Trays of seedlings are carried down the lines and a seedling is laid next to each hole. A man then comes down the line with a machete and cuts the bottom off the pots. Another gang places the pot in the hole and lines it up with the other seedlings, so everything is in neat cross rows. The planting gang then sets the coffee seedling correctly in the planting hole. The bottom of the coffee plant is set an inch higher than the surrounding ground, so the water will always drain away from the stem.

A planter then carefully removes the plastic from the pot and, with his hands, starts to fill in the earth around the seedling. As he fills in the earth, he packs it in tight. The last bits of earth are brought towards the plant with a hoe and are packed tight with his feet. This is followed by the basin makers.

A basin is a wall of earth a meter in diameter around the plant. It is to keep the water from running down the hill when the coffee is irrigated. It also helps capture the rainwater and makes sure that as much precipitation as possible can be of use to the plants. The basin makers are women and the planters are men. I am not sure why this is but no respectable man would be caught as a basin maker and vice versa. The women have a meter stick, which they lay beside the plant. With a hoe, they form a wall of earth around the plant a meter in diameter.

A worker then fills the basin with water. The water helps settle the soil and collapse any air pockets. The seedlings have been stressed with the transport to the fields and the planting process. A good soak of water helps them recover and get on their way.

Finally, one of the older women collects all the plastic from the pots and takes it away. Each gang is led by a foreman who has three or four junior foremen under him. When all goes well, at the end of the day, we look at neat rows of perfectly planted coffee and feel satisfied. We could see our farm going from bare earth to coffee plantation.

For the next two years, the plants will be weeded, irrigated, fertilized, and pampered. In their second year, they will flower with the first rains. Masses of small white flowers fill the air with wonderful fragrance. Throughout the rainy season the flowers develop into berries. As the rains leave and the colder weather arrives, the berries turn from green to yellow and finally to red. When they are red, they would be ready for picking. By this time Amy and I would be well adjusted to life as coffee farmers. But, in the meantime, we still had much to learn.

4

e quickly fell into the routine of farm life. The day begins early with a gong rung at 4:30 a.m. to wake the compound. The compound is the local term for the workers' village.

Just before 6:00 a.m., I would leave the house and head to the coffee factory. I was working hard to learn the local language and took every chance to practice it. I would greet everyone in Shona and the older workers would go through the complete traditional greeting with me. How are you? How is your family? How is your household? How are the cattle?

When I passed Rhoda and her assistant maid going to the house, I would practice more complicated sentences. They were always very polite and didn't want to correct my grammar in case it caused me embarrassment. For a whole month they were reminded to eat the dogs.

At 6:00 a.m., everyone assembles for parade. Parade sounds rather grand but it is just a term for the meeting before the start of the day. Since a lot of early settlers were ex-British army there were a lot of military terms that found their way into the farming lexicon. I am sure they were thinking, "just what the native needs, good military discipline."

A cook makes a large tub of tea and a large tub of porridge for everyone. As people assemble they have a light breakfast of tea and porridge. At 6:30 a.m., Danmore gets everyone to gather and someone leads off by singing a hymn. The hymns are in Shona and are sung with different people doing harmonies. It was always a special part of the morning for me. The singing is beautiful.

After singing, a prayer is said. The supervisor designates someone to say the prayer. It could be anyone. A typical prayer would be full of thanks and would go something like this:

> "Heavenly Father, we thank you for another day and the opportunity to be together on our farm. We thank you for the rain you sent in the night and the promise of a good crop. We thank you for our families and our children. We thank you for blessing Chipo and Mishek with another child that was born last night. We pray that you remember to look after Promise who is sick. We pray in the name of your son, Jesus Christ. Amen."

I found that Africans, both black and white, were quite religious. Our farmers' association meetings, whose membership was predominantly white, would also start with a prayer.

The Africans, however, seemed to have their own form of Christianity. They would blend mainstream Christianity with traditional beliefs. Ancestor worship was important and witchcraft was believed to be behind most ill fortune. When the Ashanti workers held a church service on the farm, it was held at night. I didn't attend any, but from the house, I could hear horns being blown and lots of chanting and singing. It sounded like a very lively affair.

After the prayer, roll call is taken. Each worker's name is read out and is answered with *pano*, the Shona word for *here*. I discuss with Danmore what jobs are to be done that day. He, in turn, instructs Jason the senior foreman to organize the other foremen and their gangs.

Samson, the farm security guard, may have an announcement to make. It could be a reminder not to brew illegal alcohol in the farm village or maybe an update on a theft case he is pursuing.

There are always a group of people hanging around waiting to see if we will need any more workers for that day. If we do, Danmore will select the number of extra people he needs. The others then walk off rather dejectedly to try their luck at another farm.

Everyone then heads out to where they are working. I go around and check that everything is going as planned and then return to the house for breakfast at 8:00 a.m. I would often see Amy returning down the farm laneway after dropping off Max for the school run. They would wait at the end of our farm laneway for one of the teachers to arrive in her pickup truck. The children would climb into the back, with the other children she had picked up along the Eastern Border road, and head off to school.

Max had just started school at our local school, Mvura Chena, which means Clear Water in the local language. Olivia would follow him there in a few years and together they would receive a wonderful elementary education. Mvura Chena was a real community effort. A local farmer had started the school instead of sending his young children away to boarding school. All the farmers and local businessmen soon pitched in and it started to grow. By the time Max and Olivia attended, it had grown into a paradise for young children. There was a stable with ponies, a large swimming pool, cricket pitch, rugby field, tennis courts and a large dam for the angling and sailing clubs. The classrooms were neatly arranged around a square with flowering trees that provided shade and beauty. There was a large hall where assemblies and plays were held and a clubhouse where they held local meetings. The clubhouse was also used by parents during sporting events. The school was a thing of great pride for the community of Chipinge.

The school was mixed-race with black children making up 60%. Farmers often paid for their children and the children of their black managers to attend the school. The rest of the students came from the families of professionals and business owners. Prior to 1980, the school system had been segregated, with the exception of one excellent private school in the capital and the famous University of Zimbabwe. They have always had a nonracial admittance policy.

At independence, all schools became multiracial. A lot of the white community, fearing a drop in standards, sent their children to private schools. The state run schools did begin to suffer from a lack of funding and by the time we were living in Zimbabwe a lot were barely functioning.

The children of our Ashanti labour force went to a school on a local tea estate. Ironically it had the same name as the private school, but where the private school used the Shona name, the tea estate school used the English "Clearwater". It was paid for and maintained by the tea estate and provided a good and affordable education.

The tea estate had built good classrooms, a sport field, and a medical clinic. It was not the same standard as the private school down the road, but it was better than the rural schools in the communal lands. The state provided the teachers and set the curriculum. The people on Ashanti were glad to have it available for their children. Most families sent their children to school, but there was a bias to give boys preference in education. I asked our gardener, who was himself well educated, why this was so. He explained that if girls go to school they can become "bitches." Even though he spoke excellent English, I was unsure I had understood correctly and asked him to explain it. He said, "An African man has pride. It would never be acceptable for him to be married to a woman who knows more than himself. It is alright for girls to go to school until grade five because all boys go to school until at least grade seven."

After breakfast, I would spend an hour in the office, then walk to the paddocks and see how the cattle were doing. The two cows Tim had given us had both given birth to calves and our little herd now numbered four. I remembered what Tim had said about cattle creating a feeling of peace and contentment. Our cattle were looking fat and content.

I would then get on a horse to check on things again. At noon, the gong rings and we break for lunch. Very few of the workers could afford a watch so one person is hired to ring the gong, a bit like the town clock. Everyone would gather at the farm community hall for lunch. We hired two cooks who cooked for the labour force. The staple diet is sadza. Sadza is cornmeal that is cooked into a stodgy substance that looks like mashed potatoes, but thicker. This is eaten with a vegetable or meat relish.

We had two full-time gardeners that tended two acres of vegetables for the lunches. A flock of 160 sheep were kept for meat. A lot of the Africans are quite deprived of protein and having lunches with a meat relish was a big hit with our workers.

After lunch I would again take a horse and go around the farm. At 3:30, the gong would sound to signal the end of the day. The work would not necessarily end then. Amy and I were also expected to be ambulance driver, magistrate, and general resolver of disputes. We were often woken up in the night to take a woman to hospital to deliver her baby or to resolve a dispute in the compound. Our role was to keep the whole Ashanti family running smoothly.

Things we needed for the farm would be purchased in the town of Chipinge. Chipinge was a mid-sized town comprised of two sections. The older part of town contained the larger stores, banks, and offices and was where the more affluent people lived. Prior to independence in 1980, this section had been predominantly white. At that time, the white population of Zimbabwe had been 250,000 people. By the time Amy and I had moved to Zimbabwe, it had shrunk to 50,000. This section of town was now home to both the white and black middle class.

The other section of town was called Gaza and was where most of the Africans lived. Gaza was a lively place of nightclubs, street soccer matches, outdoor markets, and smaller brick homes. The roads weren't paved, there was a slight smell of sewer and smoke, and the odd bit of rubbish blew down the street. There was always the beat of African music in the background, mixed with laughter and lively chatter. Only one white family lived in Gaza. The husband was an auto electrician. I visited their house once. It was after the club closed one Saturday night and everyone was invited back to their house for a nightcap. I remember, as we walked into the house, there was a wall where every guest signed their name in marker. Their relaxed ways suited living in Gaza.

We would leave our farm and drive the twenty-five kilometres to Chipinge. The last part of the drive was down a long hill to the outskirts of town. On our left we could see Gaza on the hillside, it was set back away from the main section of town of town. As we approached, we passed the Chipinge Club on the edge of town with its polocrosse fields, golf course and clubhouse.

Here the streets were lined with flowering trees; purple jacarandas, red flamboyants and flame trees. The first couple of blocks were residential. All the houses were single story with either tin or tile roofs. Some had beautiful, well-maintained gardens and others looked neglected. Some had high walls around them and others were open to the street.

The centre of town had two banks, a hotel, the town office, and two farmers' co-ops. There was also a variety of clothing stores. In fact, you could buy just about anything you needed in Chipinge. Who could have believed that within a few years this would all change and in the years following 2000, we would be lucky to get even the most basic of things?

As newcomers, what we really noticed was the number of people hanging around. People would be sitting on the curb, standing at the corners, or just slowly walking the streets. Everyone was cheerful and seemed to just like hanging around town. Ice cream salesmen would pedal bikes with coolers on the front selling Lyon's Maid ice creams. Street vendors would walk around selling cool drinks and snacks. The only people who seemed to be in a rush were the white people, busy getting what they needed, lamenting that town was becoming rather dirty, and getting back to their farms after a quick drink and bite to eat at the club. The farmers would however, slow down to catch up on the news with each other at the farmers' co-ops and Chipinge Diesel.

Farms in Africa have a large labour force. The average wage is a dollar a day and still there is high unemployment. There is every incentive to employ people. Everything on our farm that could be done manually, was. If we needed crushed stone, it was cheaper to have men with hammers break up rocks than to buy crushed stone. We had two hundred employees who lived on the farm. At peak times the number would go up to 1000. Most of these extra people would walk in from the communal lands. The Africans are cheerful, respectful and hard working.

Amy and I tried to make working at Ashanti fun. We organized social events for our workers; the most popular being soccer. Every farm had a soccer team. Our team was *The Ashanti Power*.

The first thing we had to do was to get boots and uniforms. Our neighbours considered Amy and me to be very liberal and we used to joke about them telling us not to spoil the labour. We did feel that, if the team participated in the purchase of the uniforms, they would have a better stake in keeping them in good condition. We set about involving the team in fundraising for the uniforms.

The team was given extra jobs to do on the weekends to raise money. Along the laneway there had been a row of silver oak trees that the previous owner had cut down. The team was tasked to dig out the stumps. This they diligently did but at the end of it they were still a long way from raising enough money.

We decided to raise money by having a movie night. We took our television up to the grading shed and set up the VCR. The only movie we had in the house was The Lion King which our children, Max and Olivia, watched endlessly. The soccer club collected an entrance fee at the door and everyone came in their best attire for the event. Watching TV was a real experience for a lot of the labour. Once the performance started, I returned to the house where we were having a friend over for supper.

Our friend was a retired Major from the British army and had bought a farm at the same time as we had. He was also raising money for his soccer team and I was quite keen for him to see my idea for fundraising. After dinner, we walked to the grading shed to see how the movie night had gone. The labour had enjoyed the movie alright but said they didn't want to see any more movies with National Parks animals. What they really wanted to see were war movies. The retired major thought they were quite ungrateful and suggested that if they wanted to see a war movie they should see Zulu.

After raising enough money, we bought very snazzy uniforms and entered the local farm league. The team practiced daily but we were unable to win any matches. This was put down to skullduggery on the part of the other teams. Witchcraft was implied because the others were jealous of our new uniforms. We then decided to have our own trophy and invite teams we were certain to beat to participate in our cup. I bought a cheesy plastic trophy with an angel holding a soccer ball and had "Ashanti Power Trophy" engraved on it. A select group of under-performing teams were invited to play for it.

The first match was against the Morganson Bullets. The match was played at our neighbour's farm, Morganson Farm. The Ashanti Power gave them a thorough beating. While Ashanti Power were doing their victory dance, the Morganson Bullets went to the edge of the soccer field where they had hidden sticks and knobkerries. They rushed back onto the field and gave the Ashanti Power a good hiding. The next day there were a few absentees from work, still licking their wounds from the football match. I decided that I had better go and watch the next game to see what goes on at these soccer matches.

The following weekend was a home game. The team was called "Dennis". They had taken the name from the owner of their farm. The match was to start at 2:00 p.m. Max and I went to watch the finish of the game at 3:00 p.m. When we arrived, the game had still not started. The opposing team was on the field doing stretches and large groups of supporters for both teams were behind the goal posts ready to cheer. Quite a few of the onlookers and supporters were drunk. The Ashanti supporters started singing and chanting and out of the farm church came our team running onto the pitch.

The game started. There appeared to be very few tactics in the play. There was no passing but lots of kicking the ball high in the air. Eventually, our team scored a goal. The Ashanti supporters all rushed onto the field singing, chanting and taunting the opposing team's supporters.

The occasional penalty was called and was always vigorously protested by the player in question. Red and yellow cards were handed out frequently. The other team scored a goal but the Ashanti Power managed to get another. At the end of the match Ashanti had won. There were no good sportsmanship gestures, like shaking hands. Instead, the losing team got onto their trailers and drove home with the winning team jeering at them.

The soccer season progressed and the battle for the Ashanti Power trophy continued. Referees had to be brought in from farther away because the local refs had been apparently influenced by *mushonga* and were made blind to penalties by the other teams.

The final match of the series was to be held on a soccer pitch at a local tea factory. Max and I went to watch. We arrived two hours late and saw the start of the match. The final was Ashanti Power versus Destiny Farm. At stake were the Ashanti Power trophy and quite a sizable bit of prize money. Ashanti played well, but was beaten by Destiny. As the time approached for the prize giving, I noticed that the Ashanti tractor had its engine running and had moved towards the road with the trailer. The chairman of Ashanti Power soccer team got up and announced that the winners were Destiny Farm and they would be taking home ten dollars and a wooden shield. In second place, Ashanti Power would take home the Ashanti Power trophy and two hundred dollars. The team then sprinted to the tractors and raced away with the winning team in hot pursuit. Max and I thought the confusion gave us a good opportunity to get away unnoticed and we left in our car.

The next day I gave the team a lecture on sportsmanship. Everybody looked very sheepish and promised that it would not happen again. Elizabeth, our only female foreman, said it was only because the referee was related to one of the Destiny players. Had he refereed the game fairly, Ashanti would have won, she reasoned, so it wasn't really cheating at all keeping the trophy and most of the prize money.

Elizabeth had been in charge of the storeroom. She issued the tools and spraying equipment out to the workers in the morning and made sure that everything came back in the afternoon. She had done a good job and was promoted to the position of foreman. This was not easy for her. African society is very male dominant and the men resented having a woman give orders.

On becoming a foreman, Elizabeth started coming to work wearing long flowery dresses. She had a basic education and was bright. She had been married but was now divorced. Her only child, a son, lived with Elizabeth's mother in their home area. Elizabeth supplemented her income working as a prostitute down the road from the farm in the small town of Junction Gate. In Africa, prostitution doesn't seem to have the same stigma as it does in the west. Elizabeth considered herself as having lots of short-term boyfriends who gave her money and presents. She would also sleep with some of the senior foremen on Ashanti, who would then assist her if she was having difficulties keeping order with her work gang.

During the bush war, where African nationalists fought to bring in universal suffrage and an end to white rule, Elizabeth was a *majiba*. Majibas were runners and informants for the guerillas. The Zimbabwe African National Union Patriotic Front (ZANU-PF) came to power in the first democratic election in 1980 and their leader, Robert Mugabe, became leader of Zimbabwe. Elizabeth remained a loyal supporter of Mugabe and ZANU-PF. Amy and I were happy to have a woman foreman and to see Elizabeth making a success of it.

Another popular event we held was a tug of war. Each foreman had to assemble a team. The team had to have a security guard, a tractor driver, four general labourers, two women, and one wild card player who didn't have to work on the farm. The week before the event there was lots of effort being put in by the foremen to get the strongest team and find the biggest wild card member.

The day of the event, everyone gathered on the soccer pitch. There was lots of betting among the teams and the spectators. Everyone on the farm had gathered to be a part of the event. Amy and I put up the prize money and had a large lunch prepared. We also organized lots of local beer for the party afterward. The local beer is called Chibuku. It is made from millet and has the consistency of a thin porridge and is an acquired taste. When purchased, it is still actively fermenting and the containers would swell up on the journey to the farm.

The tug of war was a round robin affair. We had a big hemp rope and the first two teams lined up. The hat was dropped and both teams heaved. The rope broke and everyone fell backwards. I couldn't believe that such a thick rope could break. We knotted it up and tried again with the same result. Our big tug of war event was turning into a disaster. A new rope was needed but, being Sunday, all the stores were closed.

Eventually a yellow nylon rope was found. It had been used to secure a submersible pump and was rough from the exposure to the elements. However, it proved strong enough though the unforgiving nature of the nylon proved to be a test of pain tolerance causing blisters and bleeding on the players' hands.

The day wore on until we were down to the last two teams in the final. Jason, the senior foreman, had one team and Samson, the security guard, the other. Jason had the technique of not pulling himself but standing next to his team and shouting encouragement. His encouragements were impressive and carried the day with a hard fought win. Jason then spent the next half hour collecting money on all the bets he had laid with the other teams and spectators. He had a most successful day and was proudly displaying a huge wad of money from his bets and his share of the prize money.

Jason had spent years working as a mine foreman and he had a natural talent for leadership. He was probably in his sixties and had no formal education. He could not read or write and his spoken English was quite poor. Yet Jason had devised clever ways to get around his lack of reading. He would memorize the order of everyone's name on the work register book. (An amazing feat since we had over 200 workers.) He would call out their names in the memorized order putting a check mark beside their names. If there was a new worker he would always ask the clerk to add the name.

Jason had also developed an uncanny feel for numbers. When there was a weeding task to be counted, he would walk down the line of bushes pointing at each one and making small movements with his lips as though he was counting. He could guess the correct number so closely that no one ever knew otherwise.

Jason could not speak English apart from a few learned phrases, which he would say in an upper class British accent. One morning his gang was repairing a roof on a house in the village. I could hear, "jolly good lads, sterling effort." I thought the retired Major was speaking until I went around the building and saw Jason.

It was months before I realized he didn't speak English. When I discussed the work to be done with him, he would listen politely occasionally saying, "yes Boss" or "very good sir, right away." He would then quietly ask someone who understood English to tell him what the job was. It was only when I had learned to speak Shona that we could finally discuss the jobs in any detail.

Like a lot African men, Jason's wife lived away in their traditional home area. Once a year, at planting time, Jason would take his leave to visit her and help her prepare their fields for planting.

The workers on Ashanti were given an area of the farm to plant their own crops. Jason's wife, Lynette, would come after the harvest to take home the corn that Jason had grown. Although they spent a lot of time apart, they had still managed to produce a large family of which Jason was very proud. Jason raised strong, hardworking girls. They would bring him and Lynette a good retirement when they married and their husbands paid the bride price, *lobola*.

Jason had, every month of his working life, deposited a portion of his wages in the Post Office Savings Bank. His wages had often been quite meager but he always made the deposit. It was growing into a nice nest egg. Even though a lot of the men working under Jason were better educated, they treated Jason with the utmost respect. The fact that he was quite tall and always carried a thick stick probably helped. Jason had lived through the various incarnations of his home, from Southern Rhodesia to the Federation of the Rhodesias and Nyasaland, to Rhodesia, to Rhodesia Zimbabwe, and finally Zimbabwe. Politics had never been of interest to him. If he did have political views, he had learned to keep them to himself. His loyalties were to his family and work.

Samson's tug of war team appeared disappointed to have lost but soon got over it and joined in the party. Samson was the head of farm

43

security. He had been in the Rhodesian army and loved to talk about his time as a soldier during the liberation, or bush war as he described it. I had thought that the conflict was pretty straightforward; the white minority was fighting to retain their privileges and the black majority was fighting to gain political power. I asked Samson why he would want to fight to keep the white minority in power. He stood at attention and replied as if addressing on officer, "Sir, we were fighting to keep the communists from destroying our country."

He then relaxed a bit and went on to tell other reasons. He described how the pay was good and how being a soldier gave him a position of standing amongst his peers. He found that he was excellent at tracking and he could navigate at night better than any of the white soldiers. He felt that there was no way the rag tag army of the guerillas, or terrorists as he called them, could ever defeat the white man. He felt he was on the winning side and his future was going to be better for it.

He described how some regiments were strictly white like the Rhodesian Special Air Service (SAS), some were predominately black like the Rhodesian African Rifles, and some, like the Selous Scouts were completely mixed. In the Selous Scouts, the white soldiers would paint their faces black and with their black peers, would pose as guerilla units. They would infiltrate the areas where the guerillas were operating to gather intelligence. After winning the trust of the genuine guerillas, the Scouts would set them up to be ambushed. Any of the survivors would be offered the chance to join the Scouts and switch sides.

After independence, soldiers like Samson had found work in the security field. When Amy and I took over Ashanti, the farm village was a mess. The previous owner had come into financial difficulties and had been unable to employ all the workers. The unemployed men found other ways of making money. Some were making moonshine and others were involved in pilfering. Samson worked hard and got the farm village cleaned up. It certainly made him unpopular with the people involved with illegal activities but the majority of the Ashanti work force appreciated the improved environment.

The next event we organized was a running race, again using the team format. A circuit around one of the fields was marked out. The race was to be a relay race with four runners on each team. The first runner from each team would run the circuit and then tag the next runner on their team, who would then run the circuit. All started out well with lots of cheering from the spectators. But then, one team developed a large lead. As it came down to the last lap, the runner on the leading team tagged his next teammate. However, all the runners started to run and it became a free for all on the last lap! As they all crossed the finish line there was much confusion and arguing over who had won. Danmore had the final say in the decision since he was the most senior worker on the farm and he rightly decided that the team who was leading prior to the last lap would be the winners.

Danmore was still a young man at thirty and it was unusual for someone his age to have such a high position on a farm. He was intelligent and determined to better himself. Danmore spoke excellent English, had his driver's license, welding license, plumbing certificate, and secondary education diploma. He wanted to get an agricultural diploma. Amy and I agreed to pay for him to do it through correspondence. He completed a three-year course in one year with excellent marks. He was fascinated by computers and was hoping to take a computer course.

His wife Chipo lived with him on the farm. They had two children, a boy and a girl. They wanted no more children and were determined to give their children the best opportunities they could. Danmore was ten years old when Mugabe came into power. Danmore, like of lot of young Zimbabweans, was disappointed with Mugabe's rule and would later be an ardent supporter of Morgan Tsvangirai, the man who would challenge Mugabe.

Tsvangirai had grown up in an area not far from Ashanti called *Ngorima*. During the latter years of the liberation war, it had become a liberated area. The Rhodesian security forces had given up trying to control it and Robert Mugabe's forces operated freely there. I assumed that people from there must have been ardent Mugabe supporters. Danmore said it had been more a matter of survival,

"The security forces would come in and accuse the people of supporting the terrorists. They would be angry and harsh with them. Then the guerillas would come and accuse the people of being sellouts to the whites. The guerillas would be very cruel and would punish someone with a horrible death as an example. The people decided they feared the comrades more. That's all."

During Rhodesian times, the farming areas were divided into commercial, African purchase, and Tribal Trust Lands. The commercial areas had been reserved for whites and were based on a freehold system of land tenure. The African purchase areas were reserved for blacks, who having completed a course on farming and being qualified as master farmers, could purchase freehold title to the land. The Tribal Trust Lands were held in trust by the state and the land was allocated by the chief to his people to cultivate. After independence, the Tribal Trust Lands were called Communal Lands in keeping with Mugabe's communist philosophies and the commercial areas were opened up for both black and white farmers.

East of Ashanti, along the Mozambican border, was a resettlement area. Prior to independence, these had been commercial farms. During the bush war these farms had been repeatedly attacked by the guerillas infiltrating in from Mozambique. The Rhodesian security forces had a difficult time providing the farmers with protection and several farms were evacuated. After independence, these farms were purchased by the state with foreign assistance to resettle black farmers and they became communal lands.

Our local chief was Chief Chivunzi. He was actually a headman ranking under Chief Mutema who was the big chief for our area. As a headman, Chief Chivunzi was Chief Mutema's representative for our local area, which covered the tea and coffee plantations along the Eastern Border Road, the resettlement area east of Ashanti, and the purchase area at the end of the Eastern Border Road.

Danmore was anxious for me to meet the chief and introduce myself as the new owner of Ashanti. We drove down the Eastern Border Road in my little Mazda pickup truck carrying a large bag of corn as a gift for Chief Chivunzi. We drove past the large tea estates with their manicured tea gardens and past Moses Machine's tea estate with his beautiful waterfall. Moses was a successful black farmer and he and his son were very active in the farming community.

We then crossed a cattle grid and entered the African Purchase area. The farms were smaller but were well run and maintained. A lot of the farmers had tea gardens and the large tea estates sent trucks daily to collect their leaf. The farmhouses were made out of brick with an accompanying traditional thatch house. There was an air of enterprise and industry and each farmer appeared to be doing rather well.

We turned off the road and bumped down a dirt track. Danmore instructed me to stop the truck and we got out. We walked a short distance and were greeted by one of Chief Chivunzi's wives, a large, obese woman. She asked us to wait while she informed the chief that he had visitors. When she returned, she led us to a grass hut. I was expecting the chief to have a larger dwelling signifying his stature in the community; however, Chief Chivunzi had a modest dwelling.

We greeted the chief with the traditional handclapping and inquired about each other's health and family. Danmore informed him that we had brought some corn and the chief sent another wife to collect it from our truck. We went into an open thatched area and sat down. Chief Chivunzi spoke no English, so Danmore acted as a translator. We spoke about the rains that had been good, about the corn that was developing big full cobs, and about the good grazing for the cattle. The chief inquired how things were at Ashanti and what our plans were. For forty-five minutes we discussed such pleasantries.

Danmore then asked the chief how he felt about the resettlement area. The chief's demeanor darkened and he looked angry. He spoke at length with Danmore and I was dying to find out what was being said. Finally there was a pause in the conversation and I asked Danmore to translate. Danmore explained how in the early days of the independence movement, a prominent figure had come from this area. His name was Dabaninga Sithole. He founded the Zimbabwe African National Union (ZANU). Robert Mugabe eventually usurped him and became the leader of the party and, at independence, the leader of the country. However, Mugabe still feared Sithole as a political rival and was using the resettlement area as a means to dilute Sithole's support base. The people being resettled were not local Ndau people, but were Karangas from Mugabe's own political base.

The Chief described how Britain had helped to purchase these commercial farms, funded a dairy scheme with imported cattle, refrigerated tanker trucks, milking parlours at each homestead, and even a state-of-the-art plant to make long-life milk. Twenty years later, there was not much left except the processing plant, which was solely supplied by the commercial farming sector. The chief said the Karangas were lazy and would rather eat the dairy cattle than have to milk them everyday. Certainly from my perspective, the resettlement scheme looked like a disaster. The land was exhausted by the continuous cropping of corn with no inputs back into the land. There was no effort made to conserve soil and the rivers flowed red with eroded soil. Any natural forest had been chopped down for firewood. The people complained that they were given inferior land and that the remaining commercial farmers were hoarding the best land.

After the chief wished us good luck with Ashanti, Danmore and I drove home. On the journey I asked Danmore what the chief's role was in the community. He explained how the chief helped resolve traditional matters such as land disputes in the communal areas, matters of traditional marriage, and matters of witchcraft. If he was unable to satisfactorily resolve the issue it was passed up to Chief Mutema.

The next day at Ashanti, one of Chief Chivunzi's sons came to apply for a job. His name was Gordon and he was well educated and extremely polite. He remained with us for four years working as a gardener, foreman, and carpenter. Sadly he developed AIDS and in the final stages of the disease, he became insane. I remember driving to the hospital with Gordon leaning out the window yelling obscenities at the people we passed. Locally, the cause of his insanity was put down to witchcraft. One of Chief Chivunzi's ancestors had become chief when another man should have and his spirit was taking revenge on the chief.

The chief would attend our annual Christmas parties and would often come to visit. We paid him to perform a ceremony to bring good rains each year. Sometimes our workers would go to him to seek solutions to their problems.

Ashanti was becoming a close community. We enjoyed seeing our farm become a fun and sociable place to work, and enjoyed getting to know the people who worked and lived with us. We were also developing a close group of friends amongst our fellow farmers.

△△△
5
▽▽▽

We got to know our neighbours. Amy joined the Wildlife Society and through the society we met Buster and Carolyn. They had a small, but beautiful farm where they grew coffee, macadamia nuts, and tobacco. Buster had won many awards for his tobacco and was considered one of the best tobacco growers in the country. He was equally well known for his drinking. He was the life of any party, engaging, witty and interesting; until the later part of the evening when things would fall apart, often ending with Buster crawling out of a damaged land cruiser that was precariously hanging over the edge of a bridge. He had an assortment of damaged land cruisers that he had unsuccessfully driven home from parties. The bridge on the road back from the club was known as Buster's Bridge.

Buster was hugely popular with the Africans. He spoke their language, understood their customs, and shared their sense of humour. Wherever Buster went, he was surrounded by Africans calling, "Mr. Buster! Mr. Buster!"

The Wildlife Society raised money for various environmental issues as well as projects to help the local communities. One of these projects was to build a new school in the communal lands. This particular school had one classroom that was old and rickety and the number of students far exceeded its capacity. The Wildlife Society raised money to build the much-needed second classroom and Buster was chosen to represent the society and present the cheque to the school committee. Buster left home in the morning and swung by the club for a quick drink before heading out to the school. Already at the club were several of Buster's friends. In no time, Buster was stuck in drinking and entertaining. It was late in the afternoon when Buster remembered his mission and dragged himself away.

Buster drove his beat-up land cruiser into the communal area and arrived at the school just as the sun was beginning to set. A huge crowd had been patiently waiting since morning and now they leapt up shouting, "Mr. Buster, Mr. Buster!"

Buster jumped out of his land cruiser clapping his hands in the traditional greeting, when a huge gasp came from the crowd. Buster had forgotten to apply the handbrake. The land cruiser was rolling down the hill, gathering speed, and heading towards the school's one classroom. It had already gone past the crowd and was moving too fast for anyone to catch up to it. Everyone stared in horror as it smashed into the classroom and demolished it.

The headmaster came to Buster with tears in his eyes, "Mr. Buster you love us too much. You would not have our children use such a bad classroom for their studies. Your commitment to further fundraising has touched us."

The next farm down the valley from Ashanti belonged to Jan Human and his son, Pete. The Africans called them *Chiranga*. Pete was dedicated to his father and continued to live at home to look after Jan. Jan and Pete were obsessed with guns. Everywhere you looked in the house there would be a gun and both Pete and his dad were incredible shots.

Amy and I leased a field of coffee from them. I would be at their farm at least once a week to check up on the coffee. As soon as I was spotted I would be called up to the house. Pete and Jan were incredibly hospitable and I would be asked to join them for a meal. They ate a lot of meals and had the physical figures to prove it.

On one occasion it was for lunch. We sat on the veranda and Pete asked if chicken would be okay for lunch. I said chicken would be very nice thank you. Pete then picked up a rifle that was close at hand and shot the head of a rooster that was crossing the garden. The cook was called to prepare it. I seem to remember it was rather tough.

On another occasion I was checking on the coffee pickers early in the morning. Pete called me up to the house for breakfast. He stood in the front doorway filling the doorframe. His huge beard made him look even larger. He boomed out, "Wilding! Get up here and have some graze," using the local slang for food.

The air became still, even the birds were silent as his voice echoed through the valley. A few of the workers giggled nervously. Jason our foreman commented using the Shona word for grazing, *kufura*, "Boss you had better go, but I hope there is lots of food or Chiranga might *kufura* you!"

We sat down at the dining room table. Pete's father Jan came into the room and sat down to join us. Pete started to clear away the various guns that were lying on the table. As he did he would hand me the odd one and say, "Dave, feel the action on this one. Isn't it nice?"

It soon developed into a real demonstration of the working parts of Pete's weapons. Guns were loaded, unloaded, cocked, and dry fired until the one I was looking at went bang and Pete's dining room window disappeared. Pete didn't miss a beat and said, "Don't worry; I have a spare glass in the shed; very sensitive action that one."

I went back down to the field and joined our workers. Jason jokingly commented that he now knows the workers who had fought in the bush war. They were the ones who threw themselves on the ground when the shot rang out.

Our neighbour to the south was another character. He had a reputation for being a very good farmer even though I never saw him in his fields. I think his real talent lay in employing an excellent supervisor. Our neighbour would head into town early in the morning under the pretense of buying a bag of cement or fertilizer. He would then proceed to the club where he would spend his day drinking. His wife had been nagging him to cut back on his drinking.

They say elephants have incredible memories and live as long as people. The old timers in our district talk of how elephants once walked from the plains of Mozambique over the mountains of Chipinge to the Zimbabwean lowveld.

One morning, an old bull elephant walked up our valley following the Chinyakonya River. It must have been seventy years since elephants had followed this route. The civil war in Mozambique, the mining of the border, poaching for ivory, the development of intensive agriculture; all these things had impacted and changed the lives of elephants.

Our neighbour was about to have his life impacted and changed by the elephant passing through his farm. He was brushing his teeth in the morning before going into town to buy a bag of cement. He looked out the bathroom window, saw the elephant, returned to the bedroom looking shocked and pale and told his wife he was quitting drinking for sure this time.

The weekends were a time to relax and enjoy some sport. Our labour force would attend a lively church service followed by a soccer match. After the match the men would head off to the local beer hall and the women would relax and gossip under the trees.

For the farmers, the Sunday social event was polocrosse. Polocrosse is a lot like polo except instead of using a mallet, a stick resembling a lacrosse stick is used. The ball can be picked up with the stick and passed in the air as in lacrosse. At the ends of the field are two goal posts through which each team tries to score a goal. Everyone in Chipinge played polocrosse. The season would start with the end of the rains at the Chipinge Club in town. The fields were well drained there and we could get on them earlier in the season.

Everyone would pitch up after church. The horses would be already there, brought in farm trucks by their drivers. The grooms would have the horses tacked up and ready to go. Usually Tim Fennel would be in charge of organizing the teams for the day. Tim would also have brought plenty of extra horses so, whether people had their own horses or not, they could play.

In the early afternoon, the waiters would come out from the clubhouse onto the field and take everyone's lunch orders. A few more *chukkas* would be played before we would retire to the clubhouse for lunch and drinks. The grooms would cool out the horses and take them home. People would stay at the clubhouse until early evening drinking, socializing and catching up on the week's events.

Later in the season, we would move to our main polocrosse club, Fiddler's Green. Fiddler's Green had two beautiful polocrosse fields and there would be two chukkas played at the same time. The clubhouse was an enormous stone building with a thatch roof. The bar area and main dining hall had fireplaces and fires would be burning there, keeping the chill out of the rooms. Even though we were in the tropics, the high altitude winters could be chilly. The bar area's walls were decorated with the skins and heads of tigers, a reminder of how a lot of the early farmers in the area had first farmed in India during the British Raj.

Davey was the black barman who ran the bar and kept the grounds immaculate. My job was to help Davey stock the bar and to assist him in keeping track of the inventory. Davey took great pride in his job and took his role seriously. There were a few members who were convinced that Davey was stealing booze to resell. I think it was more an issue of these members forgetting how much they were drinking and not keeping track of their bar tab. I never found any evidence of Davy stealing and would resent these members saying, while Davey was in earshot, "Watch that one, they all steal."

Davey didn't appear to outwardly mind and when I spoke to him about it, he would say it was what you had to put up with when you work in a bar. He said most members treated him respectfully and that there were always a few difficult people. He made note that most of the difficult people behaved that way in front of their friends. In private, they would be the first to congratulate him on the birth of a child or to drop off some extra corn for his family from their harvest.

Davey would prepare a barbeque fire in the morning so that when the last chukka had been played, people could cook the meat they had brought for lunch. Everyone took turns bringing salads and desserts.

There was an enclosed riding ring where the children could ride. Max and Olivia would ride their ponies, Pookie and Diana, along with the other children. Max soon felt he could ride out in the big field and I remember looking on nervously as this little boy, whose legs didn't go below the saddle, would come cantering across the main polocrosse field.

There were lots of committees, clubs, and organizations to be part of. Amy joined the garden club and I sat as a director for the medical clinic and the coffee mill. The Zimbabwe Coffee Mill is a cooperative owned by the Zimbabwean coffee farming community. Coffee is shipped from the farms to the mill for final grading and classification. The mill would find buyers for the coffee and promote Zimbabwe coffee.

We also provided extension services for the small-scale coffee sector. The main area for small-scale coffee production was the Honde Valley.

The Honde Valley was a good drive from the coffee mill and one entered the valley at its widest part. As we drove further in, the area became more fertile and the rainfall higher. At the very end of the valley was Eastern Highlands Estate, a large tea and coffee operation. In the communal lands around this estate there were lots of small coffee farmers..

The coffee mill would give these smaller farms pre-harvest financing, help them transport their coffee to the mill, provide fertilizers and chemicals, and advice on growing coffee. I was part of the advising group. The small-scale sector contributed very little to the overall national crop but had a significant shareholding in the mill and were an important part of any donor funding the coffee sector might receive.

In 1997 fantastic coffee prices were followed by a huge increase worldwide in the area of land planted to coffee. Everyone wanted to grow coffee and make a fortune. However, this increase in production soon led to a collapse in the coffee price. By 1999, coffee was hitting all-time low prices. The price had gone from almost four dollars a pound to eighty cents a pound and lower.

A lot of the small-scale farmers were finding coffee nonviable. In the large-scale commercial sector, only the best and most efficient farmers were making ends meet. Our Honde Valley farmers wanted to take out their coffee and plant other more profitable crops. However, we needed the small-scale sector, so we were busy giving them inducements to keep their coffee.

On a global scale a similar thing was happening. Coffee roasters were making a fortune out of the record low price of coffee. The last thing they wanted was a decrease in production, as farmers switched to more profitable crops, and an increase in the coffee price. Quite quickly, there were all sorts of things: Fair Trade, Utz Café, Coffee Kids, Shade Grown, etc., offering coffee farmers inducements to keep their nonviable coffee in. The roasters passed on any extra costs to the consumer as the extra price of buying "ethical coffee". Our Honde Valley growers and the larger coffee community, I feel, would have been much better off in the long run, by switching to other crops. It will be interesting to see what happens to these various programs when the New York Coffee Exchange futures contract, and the Coffee Sugar and Cocoa Exchange (CSCE) hits three dollars again.

6

Our green truck was packed and ready to go. There were snacks and juice boxes for the children, Barney's Big Surprise was in the tape deck and ready to play, and a tea basket was next to the passenger seat. Rhoda was sitting between Max and Olivia in the back seat bracing herself for six hours of the *I Spy* game.

In the back of the truck sat two Ashanti workers who were getting a lift to the intersection at Tanganda Halt. They were on their way to their *musha*, or traditional home, to take their annual leave. They had with them sacks filled with the corn they had grown at Ashanti.

Every year, a section of Ashanti was set aside for the workforce to use for their own crops. They were given a designated field, the use of a tractor, a certain amount of diesel, subsidized seed and fertilizer. Each worker, who would like to grow his own crops, was allotted a section of the field. The worker's committee did the allotment of the resources. It usually worked out that Danmore, as the senior supervisor, got a good-sized section of land that was plowed, disced, and the planting lines laid out. Jason, the senior foreman, would have a similar allotment just a bit smaller. The other foremen and gang leaders would have allotments that were plowed only, and so on, down to the general workers who would have a small, unplowed section. Danmore and Jason would have

59

the money to hire some people to plant and weed their sections. The general workers would have their families help them.

I would plant the farm corn crop close to where the Ashanti workers had their allotments. When the corn was ready for harvest, theft would become a big problem. Since the workers were very diligent in guarding their ripening crop, the thieves would generally pass us by.

The workers in the back of the truck had organized their sacks of corn and had settled themselves in for the journey. Amy was standing outside the kitchen smoking one last cigarette to keep her nicotine levels up until we stopped in Mutare in a few hours time. Our final destination was Harare, the nation's capital. We were going to the Vice Chancellor's Christmas party.

Graham Hill was the vice chancellor of the University of Zimbabwe. Every year, he and his wife Viv, threw a Christmas party. It was the social event of the season and everyone wanted to get an invite to it. I had met Graham and Viv on my first trip to Zimbabwe. Viv was a very active equestrian and we developed a close friendship through horses. It was Viv and Graham who encouraged us to move to Zimbabwe and take advantage of the opportunities the country had to offer young people.

Graham was a vet by profession. He had started his career inspecting cattle at the dip tanks in the communal areas. By law, cattle had to be dipped at regular intervals to prevent the spread of tick-borne cattle diseases. A dip tank is like a swimming pool for cattle. They are brought through a corral that gradually gets narrower as it approaches the pool. The cattle swim through the pool and out the other side. The water in the pool is treated to kill the ticks that feed on the blood of the cattle. Graham's job was to make sure the cattle were dipped correctly. He would also check and treat them for any other diseases and offer advice on cattle husbandry. It was all part of the government's program to assist the communal farmers in improving the health of their cattle.

Graham told me how it would be a long and dusty day in some very remote parts of the country. Even with a wide brimmed hat his skin would burn. He was amazed to learn that his black assistants and vet students also suffered from sunburn.

In the 1970s, the guerrilla war made dipping cattle in some of the communal areas too dangerous. The African Nationalists viewed the program as too paternal and would carry out attacks on the vets and villagers who brought their cattle to be dipped. In some areas the program had to be stopped.

Graham also had been teaching veterinary science at the University of Zimbabwe. UZ, as it is known, had an excellent reputation for turning out world class graduates. It had always had a nonracial admittance policy. Where the primary and secondary school system had been segregated, the tertiary system wasn't.

After independence in 1980, Mugabe himself became the ceremonial head of the university as its Chancellor. Graham became Dean of Veterinary Sciences and an expert on tropical diseases in livestock. Over the years, he moved up the ladder until he ran the university as its Vice Chancellor. Many people felt Mugabe would appoint a black man, probably from his party, ZANU-PF, to the top job. However, Mugabe felt that no one else had the skill and credentials of Graham. Refusing to bow to pressure from his party to award the top job to a political crony, Mugabe gave the job to Graham.

Graham would meet Mugabe on a regular basis to update him on university matters and Graham found him courteous and thoughtful. Often they would discuss matters not related to the university. Mugabe told Graham that his ministers would only tell him what they thought he wanted to hear. He appreciated Graham's frankness and honesty.

Viv developed a friendship with Mugabe's wife Sally. They worked together to raise funds and awareness to provide kidney dialysis for those unable to afford it.

Graham was very proud of his university and often I would go and visit him at his office. He had a spacious second floor office that looked out over the university campus. The university grounds were like a park with flowering trees and green lawns. Graham often marveled how students would come to the university having grown up in mud huts and leave as scientists and doctors.

He commented to me that during the 1970s the university was a hotbed of political activity. The black student body followed closely what the black nationalists were up to and were themselves agitating for political reforms. The government of Ian Smith made sure the university could be easily closed and any demonstration cordoned off and contained. The university was fenced and the entrances easily gated.

The Vice Chancellor's party was held at Viv and Graham's house in the northern suburb of Borrowdale. They had a spacious bungalow with ten acres of grounds. Viv had a stable for her horses and riding rings to exercise them in. In amongst the swimming pool and tennis court, Graham maintained beds of flowers and aviaries of parrots and finches, it was a gardener's dream. There were trees from Africa, South America, and Asia, There was a section that was like a jungle, another like an English garden, and one section of cactus and succulents. Graham's pride was his orchid house, under shade, the delicate plants thrived.

Inside, the house was full of antiques and one could easily believe you were in an English country house if it were not for the tropical breeze blowing through the open doors and the palm fronds brushing against the windows.

For the party, a large marquee tent was set up in the yard. Tables were laid and a little card with each guest's name on it was set in front of a plate. Guests began arriving early in the afternoon. The first to arrive were the black members of Graham's teaching staff. They arrived punctually at 1:00 as the invite stipulated. The men would be dressed neatly in jacket and tie and the ladies in dresses. They would order a coke from the bar and stand together just outside of the tent quietly talking amongst themselves.

Their conversation would start with exchanges of pleasantries and after a while move on to politics. The university lecturers were keenly aware of what was happening in the political arena. They discussed Mugabe's attempts to turn Zimbabwe into a one party state against the wishes of the people. They discussed their desire to see Zimbabwe become a multi-party democracy. Like their contemporaries in the labour movement, some of them had political ambitions of their own.

One exception was the Dean of English literature. He was a tall, good-looking man from the Ndebele tribe. The Ndebele had ruled Zimbabwe before being defeated by the British. Zeke was a direct descendent of the Ndebele king who had fought the British. He could accept their defeat to the British. He felt the British were, after all, a warrior tribe like the Ndebele.

The Ndebele had defeated other tribes and were familiar with the outcomes of both victory and defeat. Their structure, discipline, bravery, and military skill had enabled them to rule over more numerically superior tribes. So, Zeke could not so readily accept the new order of things where the Shona tribe, the Ndebele's former vassals, held power – power that was derived from numerical, rather than military, superiority. Zeke felt he had more in common with the British and was an ardent anglophile.

Zeke's passion for English literature drew him into Graham's study where he would look through Graham's collection of books. He was particularly fond of Graham and was delighted when Graham proposed him for membership in his gentleman's club, the Harare Club. The paneled walls, stuffy atmosphere, and sense of privilege were very much to Zeke's liking.

Soon other guests started to arrive. Viv and Graham had a large group of white friends from the equestrian and farming community.

Upon arriving the men and women would split up. The women would stroll through Graham's extensive gardens on their way to admire the horses in Viv's stables. The men would gather at the bar. With a Castle beer in one hand, cigarette in the other, the men would joke and tell stories.

I spotted a friend of mine amongst them and went over. David Evans was a large, good-natured man. He had been born in Tanzania where his father worked in the colonial service. He was sent to England for schooling and on completion of his studies decided he wanted to return to Africa. David applied for a job with the British South Africa Police. He went to the recruitment office in London and described the interview starting with the recruitment officer asking, "Do you know how to ride a horse?"

David replied with a touch of indignation, "Of course."

The recruitment officer then asked, "Do you have a dinner jacket?"

David replied again, "Of course."

"Jolly good then. When can you leave?" concluded the interview.

David worked in what was then Rhodesia as a police officer training the remounts. He enjoyed working with the horses but, after several years, quit to go into business.

In the 1970s, as the war with the African Nationalists was heating up, all men under the age of 65 had to do national service. Twenty years later, it was still a topic that came up a lot and men compared and discussed with each other what units they served in and what operations they had taken part in. David had served in an elite unit. He was however, not one to glorify or talk too much about the war. He told me that he was, in fact, often very afraid of being killed and one of the reasons he made sure he was in an elite unit was to ensure he was operating with trained and skillful soldiers. David felt he had a much better chance of surviving on difficult missions with them, rather than on routine operations with less well-trained soldiers.

While David believed he had a duty to serve his country, he felt they were, at best, fighting to delay what was inevitable, and, at worst, creating a climate where the more extreme elements in the nationalist movements were gaining prominence. He said the war was unpleasant and messy and that he still had nightmares about it.

One incident in particular still haunted him. He described how his unit had intelligence that a group of terrorists were at a village. The Rhodesian army's resources were stretched and they could not respond as quickly as they wanted. They arrived too late. The villagers had been locked in their huts and the huts set on fire. The sight of the corpses made David sick, but the worst was the charred bodies of children. He said their lips had been pulled back as they burnt producing a macabre smile.

I asked him if things were different for white Zimbabweans now. "In a lot of ways things really haven't changed," he answered. "We still live a very comfortable life. We have servants and lots of leisure time. The weather is conducive to sports and we have great country clubs."

"Some things have changed," he continued. "There are few whites remaining in the civil service, police, and army. We have no political power but a lot of the changes are fine. Some things had been unfair. When I joined the police I started at a higher wage and rank than a black policeman who may have had many years seniority."

I left David at the bar telling an amusing story to the group of men gathered around him. It was about a pickpocket that was hit by a car. David had to return the body to his home area. Of course the wallet wasn't his and the mistaken identity caused a series of darkly amusing twists and turns.

I caught up with Amy and we spotted our lawyer chatting with Graham. Ray was an intense man with a thick shock of grey hair. Graham had recommended Ray to us for help setting up our company and advice on the purchase of Ashanti. Ray represented and advised the university on legal matters. Graham said he was often pitted against the firebrand black lawyer, Shelby Hwacha. In court, Graham said they both had excellent legal brains and he often wondered which should be representing him.

Ray was joking about how in the past everyone wanted a white lawyer. Some of the black law firms would be tempted to include an English surname in the firm's name like; Mudiwa, Ngwena, and Smith Legal Practitioners. He said black lawyers had acquitted themselves so well and had such a good reputation that he was tempted to make his firm, Wintertons Legal Practitioners, to sound more indigenous.

Socializing together in the garden was a group from the diplomatic community. Amy and I recognized some from the Canada-Zimbabwe Society and went over for a chat. People working for aid organizations and foreign services loved being posted to Zimbabwe. It is considered a plum posting; third world enough that things are cheap but with all the amenities and luxuries of the first world.

They were discussing what they should be calling the black population. They were very concerned that whatever term they may use, would be considered racist or degrading. The common term used by white Zimbabweans, muntu, was definitely out they conferred. Muntu means "people" in the Ndebele language.

Aboriginal was discussed and considered acceptable until someone mentioned that it actually means "not part of the original." In other words, not part of the Garden of Eden. Aboriginal was discarded.

Someone mentioned African. Everyone nodded and agreed that it would work, just never shortened to Affy. "Oh, but what about the white Africans? Certainly the Afrikaners call themselves Africans," someone interjected.

"Maybe indigenous would be good," another person offered.

"Or perhaps black. We use that back home," someone from the American Embassy offered.

The leading black academics in Zimbabwe were standing not too far from us. We could have gone over and asked them for their input but everyone felt it would be inappropriate.

Someone from one of the nongovernmental organizations was lamenting that the work he was doing on improving corn production wasn't entirely having the results he wanted. He had managed to increase yields threefold – primarily through better seeds and fertilization – but he was disappointed to find out that the people he was working with were now planting two-thirds less land.

I spotted my friend, the retired Major, and went over to chat with him. He was in conversation with another man. They were having a good chat about military experiences. The topic of special forces was of interest to them both and in particular SAS, since they had both served in SAS units, one in Britain and the other in Rhodesia.

A priest came over hoping to join the conversation. He said that, as a Jesuit, he was one of God's SAS. As the conversation predictably petered out, Graham's wife, Viv rang a bell. She announced that before the meal was to be served, there was going to be a little competition.

Viv cleverly organized everyone into teams, mixing up all the little groups of people. The first part of the competition was a scavenger hunt. The different teams went through the garden collecting things on the list. Once that was finished, the teams sat down at their allotted tables. There was a general knowledge quiz and the competition finished with each table singing a Christmas carol.

David Evans in his deep baritone voice helped his table win by belting out, "I'm Dreaming of a White Christmas." He then turned to the black people on his team and with a wink said, "Some of us still are!"

Viv's competition was a great icebreaker and by now everyone was joking and having a wonderful time. Graham made a speech thanking everyone for coming. He told a funny story about his early days as a vet, thanked his university staff, and wished everyone a Merry Christmas.

Much too soon the sun began to set on Graham's gardens and the insects of the night began their calls. Graham's university staff had gone home and a few people remained at the bar. Amy and I went to thank Viv and Graham for a lovely day. We had met so many interesting people, all who shared a love for Zimbabwe.

As I was shaking Graham's hand good-bye, he held on to it and said with such sincerity, "David, Viv and I are so glad you and Amy have come to Zimbabwe. This is a very special place. Everyday you feel alive. Everyday is an adventure. It offers you so much opportunity to make a difference. A difference to yourself and to others. I have been able to do so much more with my life here than I would have been able to do anywhere else. I am so proud of this country and all its people. And I am so proud of what it can still achieve in the future."

7

*A*round this time an event was taking place that would have huge consequences for all of us, even though none of us had any idea of the significance of it yet. In fact, events would unfold that would leave Zimbabwe forever changed.

An alliance of church groups, human rights groups, civic organizations, journalists and lawyers had formed to campaign for constitutional reform. They called themselves the National Constitutional Assembly (NCA). Workshops and consultations were held across the country to allow the people to voice their ideas on what they wanted in a new constitution. People eagerly presented their ideas. There was widespread consensus on the need for electoral reform, limits on presidential terms, and independence of the media, police and judiciary.

Zimbabwe's long-serving president, Robert Mugabe, had changed and altered the existing constitution to suit him and his party, the Zimbabwe African Nationalist Union-Patriotic Front (ZANU-PF). He had granted himself more and more powers and adjusted the electoral rules to make it hard for another party to successfully challenge him. He felt the best way to counter this new threat to the existing constitution was to do his own exercise in constitutional reform. In 1999, he set up the Constitutional Commission of Inquiry, which duly presented a draft constitution favourable to him. Mugabe then inserted his own clause into it. By special gazette, he added an amendment allowing him to expropriate farmland without compensation. He felt that this would be popular with the poor black population. The result would show how much Mugabe had was losing touch with the people. Mugabe's draft constitution was taken to the people to vote on in a referendum. The NCA, seeing that their exercise had been hijacked, encouraged the people to vote against it.

The people rejected the proposed constitution in the referendum. It was the first time, since independence in 1980 that the people had voted against the wishes of the President. It gave Zimbabweans a renewed interest in politics and confidence that they could effect change.

Mugabe himself appeared on television. He described the result as "unfortunate" but went on to declare, "Let us all accept the verdict and plan the way forward."

Mugabe made note of the peaceful nature of the referendum and mentioned the upcoming parliamentary elections, "The world now knows Zimbabwe as a country where opposing views can file so singly and so peacefully to and from the booth without incident. I have every confidence that the forthcoming elections will be just as orderly, peaceful, and dignified. May I also make mention of the white part of our community who this time around sloughed off apathy to participate vigorously in the whole poll."

Everyone should have paid more attention to his visibly shaking hands that held the script and the tightness of his mouth. They were the only indication of the rage he felt and the recriminations that lay ahead.

At this time a new political party was emerging. The Movement for Democratic Change (MDC) had its roots in the labour movement. It quickly gained popularity with a population increasingly tired of

Mugabe's autocratic and corrupt leadership. Many whites, who had stayed out of politics since Independence in 1980, started to get involved with politics again. The educated professional black class, the young, and the urban population all got behind the party. On our farm the new party was causing a lot of excitement. Danmore and a lot of our younger workers were taking a big interest in what Morgan Tsvangirai, the MDC leader, had to say. Even Jason who had always shunned politics would smile when people would call out the MDC slogan, *Change your ways. Chinja maitero! (Support the movement!)*

The forthcoming elections that Mugabe had mentioned in his speech were the parliamentary elections to take place in 2000. The MDC were going to field contestants. This was the first real threat to Mugabe's rule in twenty years and he began a plan to crush any opposition. Mugabe and his ruling elite feared the loss of power. They feared the loss of their salaries, perks, commissions, bribes, and contracts. They feared being held accountable for past atrocities.

The referendum gave him a picture of which areas still supported him and which supported the opposition. The urban population, the professional classes, and students supported the No vote. The rural population in the communal lands provided some support for the Yes vote. The population in the commercial farming areas had supported the No vote.

Mugabe's objective was to destroy the opposition and all those that supported it or had the potential to. He declared, "No matter what force you have, this is my territory and that which is mine I cling to unto death."

In the commercial farming areas, his plan was to disperse white farmers and their workers through the guise of land reform. It was to be portrayed as an uprising by land-hungry veterans of the liberation war who were to take back the land that the ancestors of the white population had dispossessed them of in the 1800s. This would cripple the farmers financially so they would be unable to finance the opposition and would have the added benefit of putting his supporters in opposition areas. It would effectively deny the MDC a large block of voters. The farm labour community were ardent supporters of the MDC.

He made racially inflammatory remarks that white farmers owned 70 percent of the land in Zimbabwe. The reality that whites owned just half of the commercial farmland, which is 14 percent of Zimbabwe's total land, was never mentioned by the free media or even by the farmers' union. This played right into Mugabe's hand. He then pushed a law through Parliament that stated you could only vote in the area where you were registered. By forcing farm workers from their home areas, he would, in effect, disenfranchise them, causing the MDC to lose a large voting block. Farm workers and their dependents numbered two million people. This plan was to be led by veterans of the liberation war. Over the next ten years, these war veterans would become Mugabe's shock troops. Most of them were not actual war vets but instead a ragtag mixture of unemployed youth, hired thugs, and riffraff. The majority was not yet even born during the Liberation War. They were to become known, not as war vets, but as *wovits*.

The wovits were sent out to put pegs on commercial farms signifying government ownership. The guise that they were land hungry peasants was quickly dispelled as it became obvious that government and army trucks were used to transport them to the farms, that they were being supplied by the government with rations, and being paid allowances. The police, army, ZANU-PF officials, and Central Intelligence Organization (CIO) agents were actively directing events.

One morning, our supervisor came to me and said the veterinarians were at Mr. Gifford's farm. I assumed a foot and mouth outbreak or some animal health issue had occurred and thought nothing more of it! Later in the day we began to hear broadcasts over our farm radios that wovits and members of the army dressed as peasants, were escorting actual peasants and putting pegs on people's farms. They would then proceed to build huts and take up residence. Rhoda, our Ndebele nanny, looked at these huts and said with scorn, "Eee Boss, in Matabeleland, even chickens would not live in them. A Ndebele chicken has higher standards than these Shona wovits. These wovits are not just eaters of dirt, they are criminals."

Rhoda went on to explain to me that traditionally the Ndebele were herders of cattle and would exact tribute from their vassal tribes. They viewed the farming practices of their vassal Shonas with disdain and referred to them as eaters of dirt. She also explained that during the liberation war, criminals fleeing from the law, would cross over the border and join the guerillas to escape justice. They were not all noble freedom fighters.

Later in the week, a group came to our farm and put some pegs in the back field. One of them was armed with a pistol. Nobody was certain how to handle this. The government claimed it was a peaceful protest; the police were instructed not to interfere with the wovits and the farmers hoped it would all pass over. I decided to confront them.

I walked out to where the wovits had camped and told them that I had just bought the farm and I certainly hadn't bought it for them. They said that they had been forced to come and put in the pegs. I realized that the pistol, carried by the one, wasn't to scare me but to force the wovits to do the pegging. I removed the pegs and took down a hut they had started to build. They left peacefully.

I was surprised to see a particularly large hut being erected on our neighbour's farm. It dwarfed the other huts that the wovits were building. I asked Danmore about it and he said it belonged to Chief Chivunzi. Having met Chief Chivunzi on previous occasions, I was surprised because he didn't seem to support Mugabe or his policies and did not live in a manner grander than everyone else. Danmore explained that during Rhodesian times, the Prime Minister Ian Smith, treated the traditional chiefs well and hoped to win support amongst the rural population through them. Danmore said that Mugabe, after neglecting the traditional chiefs during his first years in power, was now doing the same and had increased the government stipend they received. "Chief Chivunzi loved Mr. Smith maybe now he loves Mugabe, but only a man himself knows what is truly in his heart," said Danmore. "Maybe this chief thinks it is better for Mugabe to believe that he is loved by this chief and leave his people alone. At elections the people can reveal their heart."

In other parts of the country things were not so peaceful. The police and army were actively and visibly involved. Farmers who tried to stop them were arrested or beaten. More disturbing, farmers were being killed by the State.

A farmer in Macheke, Dave Stevens, and his foreman, Julius Andoche, had a confrontation with wovits who were camped out on their farm. Together with the farm workers, they evicted the wovits. But the wovits returned with a busload of reinforcements. Dave tried to talk to the wovits. They beat him and tied his hands behind his back. They burnt farm buildings, looted his house and drove off with Dave. Five of Dave's friends arrived and followed the convoy that was carrying him. As the convoy was approaching the local ZANU-PF headquarters, a wovit leaned out of a vehicle and opened fire on Dave's friends. They went into a police station hoping for protection. They were dragged out of the station by the wovits. The police stood by and watched.

After beating Dave and trying to drown him in a puddle, the wovits shot him in the back of the head. Julius Angoche was also shot dead. The other farmers were beaten throughout the night and then dumped in the bush. No one was convicted of the murders.

A few days later a farmer in Bulawayo, Martin Olds, had his homestead surrounded by about a hundred armed men that had been transported to his farm in a thirteen-vehicle convoy. He called the police for assistance, but was told it was political and they could not respond. Not only did the police not respond, they blockaded the road to his farm and prevented his neighbors from coming to his assistance. He went out to negotiate with the wovits and was shot in the leg. He managed to get back into his house and for the next three hours he held off the attackers. His friend, Guy Parkin, tried to go to his assistance but was driven off by gunfire. When the thatch roof of his house caught on fire, Martin filled a bathtub with water, immersed himself and went back out to return fire. Eventually, with his house ablaze, he was forced into the open and shot and killed. The attackers then spent the next two hours removing cartridge cases and other evidence. They then drove back through the police blockage waving weapons and singing songs. Nobody was ever arrested.

Any doubts about the State and Mugabe's involvement in the attacks were gone when, later that day, Mugabe made the following statement at a news conference, "They're (the white community) mobilizing, actually coercing, their labour forces on the farms to support the one position opposed to government, has exposed them as not our friends, but enemies. Our present state of mind is that you are now our enemies because you really have behaved as enemies of Zimbabwe".

Of course, anybody connected to the MDC were enemies in the eyes of Mugabe. Black commercial farmers were also evicted from their farms. One such farmer, Philemon Matibe, ran for parliament as an MDC candidate and feeling he unfairly lost challenged the results in court. He was told that if he dropped his petition he would be allowed to continue farming. He refused to drop his case. The district administrator and a mob of eighty wovits arrived in a convoy of vehicles and drove him from his farm. Philemon summed it up, "This is not about correcting colonial imbalances. This is about punishing your enemies."

Our farming community held a memorial service at our Dutch Reform church in Chipinge for the murdered farmers. We were all starting to get worried. Plans were made to evacuate to Mozambique if things got worse. The men were organized into security groups. Roll call was held over the radio in the evening. Each farm was announced and the farmer would reply that all was well. This was followed by a situation report updating everyone on the situation in the country. Amy and I were given a farm radio by Tim so we were able to stay in contact with other farmers and be able to do the roll call and hear the "sitreps" (situation reports). It seemed as though every couple of weeks another farmer was killed. Mugabe was killing enough farmers to keep everyone scared, but not so many as to force the international community to intervene. There were rumours that a farmer would be killed in every district. We all wondered who it would be in our district. There was a fear that things could degenerate even further.

Of course, it was not just the farming community that was being intimidated. Teachers and other professionals were singled out for beatings and "re-education". Teachers were dragged before their students, humiliated, and beaten. Their homes and property were destroyed and many were forced to flee for their safety. By May of 2000, two hundred-and-fifty schools had been forced to close and seven thousand teachers had fled.

Mugabe felt threatened by the business community. A government source told the weekly paper, *The Financial Gazette*, "The President is especially annoyed that business is condemning the policies of his government and party."

Wovits invaded businesses, assaulted the workers and extorted money from the owners.

Even more sinister and evil things were in the making.

ZANU-PF began training its activists to systematically disrupt MDC activities and to eliminate MDC members and candidates. The activists were taken to King George VI Barracks in Harare for training. They were taught techniques of assassination, arson, and political indoctrination. Upon graduation, a large ceremony was held at the Sheraton Hotel. Robert Mugabe gave their upcoming mission the name "Operation Tsuro" (tsuro meaning hare in Shona) and made it very clear what was expected from them, "When we are speaking of the struggle, we are talking about killing people so the country can be free. If one of you is asked why you are killing, you say it is not us, it is the President. But we behave like hares. The baboons have a big build, but the hares are more clever."

Everyone realized that the upcoming election would be crucial to the survival of the farming community and Zimbabwe. One of our local farmers, Roy Bennett, was going to run for parliament. He was a fluent Shona speaker and a leading figure in the community.

As the election got closer, things got hotter. Wovits and youth from Mugabe's Youth Brigade started to beat up anyone linked to the opposition. Farm invasions increased and more farmers were killed. People began to question if it was the right thing to challenge Mugabe. The parliament has a number of seats that are appointed by the president. Could the opposition win enough seats to still have a majority with these appointed seats? What would be the extent of vote rigging? Since the presidential elections take place separately two years later, would a parliamentary win make any difference?

What made people remain resolute was the massive support that the opposition seemed to have among the people. The symbol of an open hand, as opposed to Mugabe's closed fist began to appear everywhere. There was a feeling in the air that history was going to be made.

On voting day, our workers were all anxious to go and cast their ballot. We arranged for them to take the tractor down the road to the hamlet of Junction Gate where the voting was to take place in the school. They left the farm with much singing and fanfare. The trailer was overflowing with people. I was afraid they would roll over going down the hill. They were shouting "Chinga Maitero" (Change Your Ways) and "Tapura Jongwe" (Pluck the rooster). Mugabe's symbol was the rooster.

The next day, we listened intently for the results to come in. The first results had the opposition winning all the announced constituencies. There was a feeling of jubilation on the farm. The people who had radios brought them with them to work and whenever another constituency was won by the opposition MDC a cheer would go up. Roy Bennett, the coffee farmer, won his seat. Then there was a period of no more announcements. We waited for the announcement of results to continue. When they did the results were mostly wins for Robert Mugabe's ZANU-PF party. The end result was the MDC didn't win a majority.

There were accusations of vote rigging, intimidation, and other forms of electoral fraud. However, the opposition MDC had made an historical showing. The multiracial, multi-tribal, political party MDC had run on a platform of change from the old ways. They had taken on Mugabe's ZANU-PF and, against enormous odds, almost won a majority.

Morgan Tsvangirai captured the mood of the nation when he said, "We want to thank a number of people, first and foremost the people of Zimbabwe for showing incredible determination to cast their votes. We bow our heads in sadness at the loss of 31 brave people who stood their ground for democratic ideas. Our hearts are filled with sadness at the tremendous losses their families have experienced and the incredible trauma to their wives and children. We have been moved by the commitment of those families to continue to support the MDC and the quest for peace and freedom in this land.

"We thank those that have died, been beaten or raped, destroyed, or they themselves and their families displaced for continuing their commitment. Their sacrifices have been considerable and we are in awe of their courage...civil society which had become moribund for twenty years has reawakened, there is a new energy and a new purpose."

In two years time, the Presidency would again be up for grabs and the MDC felt confident they would win it.

I did wonder why Mugabe would go to the trouble of holding elections when he clearly had every intention of rigging them and ensuring he and ZANU-PF would emerge the winners. He appeared to have no intention of relinquishing power. Would it not make more sense for him to do away with elections altogether?

Roy Bennett, the coffee farmer who had just won a seat in parliament, had also been awarded "Coffee Grower of the Year." To win this prestigious award you have to excel in all aspects of coffee farming; yields, cup quality, labour practices, environmental practices, soil conservation, and long term planning. The recipient hosts a field day to enable other coffee farmers the chance to learn, ask questions, and improve their farming techniques.

At Roy's field day, the questions quickly turned to politics. Politics had become foremost in everyone's mind. The question of why Mugabe would bother to go through the motions of elections, when he clearly considered himself the only God chosen leader to rule, came up.

Roy explained, "We have to go back to 1980, the year of Zimbabwe Independence."

Some of the farmers were too young to remember much from 1980 and others, like myself, had not lived in Zimbabwe at that time.

"Robert Mugabe and his party, ZANU, had been fighting a war of liberation from colonial domination supported in that cold war era by China. ZANU's leaders were deeply skeptical about participation in elections because they believed elections would be rigged against them. ZANU was forced into this election by their main guerrilla host sponsors, Mozambique and Tanzania. ZANU participated reluctantly and angrily yet they also came up with a plan to ensure a manufactured majority of Zimbabweans would vote for them. Advised and trained by Peking at the time, they did this by terrorizing and brutalizing the rural population, which then, as now, constitutes the bulk of our people.

"Terror was not new to Mugabe's Zimbabwe African National Liberation Army (ZANLA). These guerrilla forces operated largely in the Shona-speaking areas of Zimbabwe during the liberation war. They relied heavily on Mao Tse Tung's strategy of terror. Arbitrary killings were the chosen means of putting fear into the innocent, defenseless rural peasant. One of the many techniques was to force so-called sellouts or collaborators to lie on the ground while their family members were forced to beat them to death. Others were tied with wire and shot at point-blank range. One terrible instance remains raw in my mind. These liberation heroes took a metal bar, heated it red hot, made a crook at the end of it, and disemboweled a woman. Her young daughter was buried alive alongside her. The whole village was forced to watch.

"Under the ceasefire arrangement at that time, Mugabe's ZANU was obliged to lay down arms and gather its forces at designated assembly points. Instead, ZANU assembled only a portion of its cadres and instructed the rest to remain at large to intimidate the people and thus guarantee the rural vote. These combatants moved among the villages and the people were told they would be shot, or have their throats cut, if they did not vote for Mugabe. Against the background of war and its sickening violence, people needed little convincing that the threat of death was real. But this did not prevent ZANU from rein-forcing the point: many more alleged sellouts were butchered during the ceasefire. Shona rural areas in Zimbabwe were no-go areas for other political parties. In one of many examples, Francis Makombe, a candidate representing the rival nationalist party ZAPU was last seen having hot coals shoved down his throat.

"Mugabe won a majority. To his surprise and delight ZANU inherited the breadbasket of Africa. International recognition, admiration and aid followed. He and his party had learnt a lifelong lesson: elections confer legitimacy, no matter how they are won. In other words, violence could always guarantee power in a so-called democracy, just as it does during war."

Amy and I, having grown up in Canada, took democracy for granted. In fact, I often hadn't bothered to vote in Canada. It was interesting and inspirational for us to see the sacrifices that Zimbabweans were prepared to make for this right. We would never again be complaisant about democracy.

8

*O*ur Ashanti workers got over the disappointment of the rigged election results, but not before sorting out a few things on the farm. The Central Intelligence Organization (CIO) had informers scattered throughout Zimbabwean society. Often they were ordinary people paid a few dollars to provide names of MDC supporters. Sometimes they may have had some training and, if called upon, could be used for intimidation purposes.

We had one rather loud-mouthed worker on the farm. Our foreman said the only part of that worker's body that wasn't lazy was his mouth. It was discovered that this man had been trained as part of the ZANU-PF youth militia and he was quickly chased from the farm.

Our mechanic and one of our tractor drivers were fingered as being too pro-Mugabe and too involved with the local ZANU-PF party. Our workers wanted them to leave the farm. They were soon caught stealing diesel from the tractors by a local policeman. They were charged and a court date set. They went to the ZANU-PF office in Chipinge and asked ZANU-PF to intercede. The policeman was transferred, the magistrate didn't want to hear the case, and the trial was remanded several times. Ultimately, after starting contempt of court proceedings, they were tried, convicted, and legally evicted from the farm only to miraculously avoid the penal system and become wovits invading our neighbours' farms!

Meanwhile, our farming operations were growing. The owners of the farm next to us, Sweet Acres, decided to emigrate to New Zealand. They were concerned about the situation in Zimbabwe and being white Zimbabweans felt that their children should have another passport. There was a fear amongst white Zimbabweans that, if things should go the way of so many other African countries, they would not be able to leave and live elsewhere. Having a second passport from a desirable country was becoming an obsession.

Our neighbours wanted to go and work in New Zealand long enough to qualify for citizenship. They then hoped to return to their farm. They leased us their farm for eight years. Interesting enough, when they had settled in New Zealand, they heard their youngest child speaking Shona to someone at the door who turned out to be the black mailman. Obviously it was both black and white Zimbabweans who were trying to get a second passport!

Having Sweet Acres was a real boost to our operations. On Ashanti we had just the basic infrastructure for coffee farming; a pulpery, homestead and workers village. Sweet Acres had an extensive workshop, store, abattoir and community hall. We had the use of three tractors, which made a big difference to us. There was a lot of work to be done on the farm. We planted more coffee and were able to double our acreage of coffee. We re-plastered and painted the buildings.

A friend of ours who was a single mother and worked in the administration department of a corporate coffee estate moved into one of the homesteads. She did a great job painting and decorating.

We got the store fully stocked and started putting animals through the butchery. Food was becoming scarcer as agricultural production started to decline with the disturbances on farms and our fully stocked store and butchery was a big hit with the workers. We also had a nice plantation of macadamia nuts on Sweet Acres. The sheep grazed amongst them and kept them beautifully trimmed.

Our little herd of cattle was growing. We borrowed a Jersey bull from Pete Human. The bull gave some lovely calves to our Friesian cows. The herd contently grazed in the paddocks that would next year be used as drying space for the coffee. Pete would drop by every so often and we would lean on the fence and watch the cattle. We would talk about cattle, farming, and life in general. The cattle looked fat and content.

The coffee on Ashanti was now two years old and had given us our first little crop. The next year's crop would be the big one. We picked the ripe cherries (the seeds inside become the coffee beans) and they were taken with the tractor to the pulpery. There the tractor tipped them into a hopper. A pipe brought water to the hopper and the water carried the cherries into the pulper. There the cherries would be squeezed through four turning disks and the skin and fruit pulp would fall down and be taken away to the skin tank. The beans would be directed into large open concrete tanks. Here they would ferment for a day.

The fermentation process breaks down the mucilage on the bean. The beans are then washed three times in the tank. They are then pumped up to our grading channel. The grading channel is like a sluice box. The water flows down carrying the beans. The heavier beans don't travel as far as the lighter beans and we are able to separate out the different grades; heavies, lights and floaters. Max and Olivia loved playing at the pulpery and the grading channel was like a waterslide.

The beans are then carried out to dry on sheets of plastic. The plastic keeps them off the ground and, at night or when it rains, the plastic can be folded over to keep the beans dry. After two weeks, the beans are dry enough to be put into bags and stored. They still have a papery skin on then that is hulled off prior to export. Our two-year-old crop was a good way to get our systems worked out before the big crop the following year.

We spent the next rainy season preparing for the first big crop. The fermentation tanks were fixed up, new disks put on the pulper. We had an old man make winnowing baskets for the women to use for grading the coffee. Roads were repaired so the tractors could get the cherries up to the pulpery after they were picked The coffee trees were carrying an enormous crop. We had to fertilize every two weeks so the trees could have the nutrients to hold the crop. As the rains neared their end we began to irrigate. One day Oliver, our foreman at the pulpery, said to me, "The rain wants to go now; the coffee will be ready soon. This coffee is going to be too much!"

The Africans use the term "too much" to mean a lot and he was right. We were soon unable to keep up with the picking.

Danmore went to speak to some of the local schools to see if they would like to come and pick coffee for us. The schools are terribly underfunded and Danmore thought that they may want the extra money to get school supplies. The first school he spoke to agreed to come. They arrived and picked coffee. We provided all the pickers and farm workers with a lunch everyday. On this particular day it was lamb and sadza (corn porridge). Everyone was very grateful as a lot of people cannot afford to buy meat often.

However, later that day, the headmaster of the school came to Danmore and said that a group of the students were sick and that the meat had been poisonous. No one else was sick, but I told Danmore that we could take them to the hospital in Chipinge to be checked out. He left with the children in our pickup truck. When he arrived at the hospital the headmaster refused to let the children get out. He said they did not want to go in.

Danmore then took them to the private clinic in town. Again they refused to get out and the headmaster told Danmore that they had to go to a doctor that Danmore had never heard of. He called me at this point unsure of how to proceed. When I spoke to him he said the children did not appear to be sick and he thought something odd was up. I told him to return to the school as we had given them two chances to seek medical help and they had refused it.

The next day a letter was brought to us by the headmaster and a local ZANU-PF official. It was written by the doctor that the headmaster had wanted the children to see. It stated that the children had been poisoned on our farm and that we had to pay compensation. Danmore was furious as it was an obvious attempt at extortion. We refused to pay anything and said that if they felt they had been wronged it must be taken to the police. Nothing further came of it but I told Danmore that I didn't want to try any more schools for picking.

A week later Danmore came to me and suggested we try another school. I was against it, but Danmore insisted that I at least speak to the delegation that was waiting to see me. As a keen learner himself, Danmore was always interested in helping people trying to get an education. They had walked four hours to come and see us. I went up to the coffee pulpery and met them. There was the *kraal* head, who is the area's sub chief, the school headmaster, the chairman of the school and the school committee. They were dressed in suits and explained that they were from Maundwa in Risitu Valley. The Risitu Valley is the ancestral home for a lot of our workers. They explained that their school had been burnt down through an arson attack. I asked who would do such a thing and they said, "a psychomaniac."

I thought that it sounded like a pretty dangerous type of person. They went on to say that the police were now looking for him as he had been declared an "unwanted man" as no one wanted him. They wanted to rebuild their school and were proposing to bring the students, parents, and school supporters to pick coffee.

We really took a liking to them and realized that they were sincere and not at all like the previous school. We arranged with a local trucker to send a truck to Risitu Valley to collect the children in the morning. The road to Risitu Valley is horrendous. It is a gravel road that has been badly washed out in many places. It drops down from the commercial farming areas into the communal lands. Some farmers help maintain the upper section of the road but beyond that there is no maintenance. Amy and I find it difficult to drive our four-wheel drive vehicle down it and I was concerned about a truck going down. However, the next morning we heard the sound of a truck arriving at the farm.

It was full of the Maundwa school people. They were singing and laughing. The truck came to a stop and they leapt out. The headmaster organized the children into a line and they were introduced to their foremen for the day. Jason felt that working with the children would be an ideal opportunity for some of the better Ashanti workers to develop foremen skills. Jason called them junior foremen. The parents formed another group and they headed off to pick coffee. They had also arrived with a small group of security guards. The headmaster explained to me that they feared that the psychomaniac would try to sabotage their efforts to rebuild the school. I could never figure out why the psychomaniac would be so determined to destroy Maundwa School. Every time I tried to get to the bottom of it the headmaster would just shrug his shoulders and say, "He is a psychomaniac."

The guards were armed with bows and arrows and slingshots. The psychomaniac turned out to have a name, Tongai Moyana. He claimed to be war vet, but anyone behaving as a thug or criminal claimed to be a wovit hoping they would be above the law. Mugabe had instructed the police to not interfere with the wovits and their activities.

Twice, Moyana hid by the side of the road to attack the children. The first time, the truck carrying the schoolchildren had to slow down going up the hill. Moyana jumped on the truck with a machete and cut three of the students. Before the guards could get to him, he jumped off and ran away. The second time the guards were more alert and prevented him from getting on the truck.

Moyana once arrived as Danmore and I were paying the coffee pickers. He was brandishing a machete and threatening to kill everyone. Danmore quietly slipped away and got word to the police. However, by the time they arrived, Moyana was long gone. We had a good idea where he had gone, but the police were unable to find him.

On another occasion, he was seen passing through our farm early in the morning. Danmore and I drove to the station and brought back a group of policemen. They spent a lot of time clearing their weapons and issuing ammunition. By the time we got onto Moyana's track, he was well ahead of us and in the end we lost his tracks.

Several years later, when Amy and I were visiting the school, I asked what had ever happened to him. We were told that when they found him, Moyana was surrounded by the people, and he committed suicide.

The Maundwa School people were a pleasure to have with us and, without them, we would have really battled to get our coffee crop off. Amy and I were impressed with their efforts to get the school built. At the end of the picking season, we matched their picking money with a grant and sent the farm carpenter to reconstruct the school. We also had blackboards made and bought basic school supplies. We developed a strong friendship between Ashanti farm and Maundwa School that continues to this day. Later, when things became very tense with the political situation, they were a huge help to us. The next year another school joined us. Ndiandzo School is the sister school to Maundwa and they also wanted to improve their school with money generated through coffee picking.

It is quite an experience to visit these rural schools. The students are neatly attired in school uniforms, even though their parents can hardly afford to wear decent clothes themselves. The children study in very rudimentary classrooms with over fifty students in a class. Two students will share a slate because paper and pens are not in the budget. There never seems to be an issue of discipline and the children diligently work at their studies. They hope an education will provide them with a bright future.

Sadly, there are few jobs in the formal job market. The official unemployment rate is 80%. We would have people come to our farm with high school diplomas showing excellent marks, but we could only offer them jobs as labourers.

*A*s the date for Presidential elections drew closer, the atmosphere in the country became electric. On Ashanti, Danmore would hand out the country's only independent daily newspaper to anybody who was interested in following the campaigning. The workers would rush up to grab the papers. I was impressed by their desire to be informed and the newspapers were recycled to roll cigarettes. Our workers would go off and attend MDC rallies. ZANU-PF would send wovits around to coerce people into going to their rallies. Elizabeth, our lone ZANU-PF supporter, was starting to feel lonely and was thinking about voting for the MDC.

Everyone was getting busy. The wovits were busy threatening that ZANU-PF would go to war if they lost the election. Our neighbours, Pete Human and his father, were busy sighting in their guns. Mugabe was busy revoking the accreditations of foreign election observers (other than the ones from countries he considered sympathetic to ZANU-PF). ZANU-PF youth militia were busy unleashing a wave of terror. The police were busy banning MDC rallies. Human rights organizations were busy trying to record abuses and not be expelled from the country. Roy Bennett and Morgan Tsvangerai were busy campaigning. The head of the defense forces was busy declaring that the military would not recognize the results if Mugabe lost. The Registrar-General was busy denying the MDC access to the voter's roll. Everyone was busy and the stage was being set for the most important election in Zimbabwe's history.

Morgan Tsvangerai and Roy Bennett came to the Chipinge Country Club and each made an impassioned speech. They filled everyone with a sense of hope and gave people confidence to resist fear and be involved with political change, even though Roy was having an increasingly difficult time on his farm with ZANU-PF mounting a full-scale invasion and his supporters resisting it.

Our farmers' association decided that they would help with the monitoring of the election. Each political party was allowed to have two members present at the polling booth to watch for rigging. They were to record the number of people going in to vote, to ensure that their numbers matched the number of votes cast. They would also record any suspicious behavior. We would be helping them move to the polling booths, supplying them with food and water, and delivering their voter attendance records to the central command post. After the voting, we were to follow the ballet boxes to where they were to be counted. A command post was to be set up at the country club to coordinate things. The retired Major from the British army was to run the command post. He would be in radio contact with everyone and monitor our movements. He had a group on standby at the command post that he could dispatch to aid anyone in trouble.

When the voter attendance results came in, a group of volunteers would email the results to another centre that would be receiving results nationwide. Everything had to be kept secret because the Central Intelligence Organization (CIO) would try to close us down if they knew where we were located – not that our country club in the middle of town could be considered an ideal hiding place. There was nothing illegal in what we were doing, but the feeling was that Mugabe would be attempting massive electoral fraud and would be using the CIO to assist him.

We were organized in pairs. My partner was Alg Taffs. Alg and his brother Charles farmed the other side of town. Both were big, gruff, hard smoking men. Alg had done a stint in the British army and had fought in the Gulf War. I thought he was a good choice of partner and jokingly said that if things got tense I was sure that the military training could come in useful. Alg told me that he would probably end up having to save my life.

The day before the election, we went to pick up the people who were acting as monitors and help get them in place for the next day. Amy had organized food and coffee for us. Alg brought along five packs of cigarettes and a book of jokes for us to read. We left early in the morning to go to the command centre to receive our monitors. It was pouring rain when we left and the wipers on my truck were not working properly. One wiper would only go up and down a little ways so I had to keep my head very close to the dashboard to see out of the windshield. As we were going down the hill past the school Alg grabbed the wheel and turned it. I had been heading off the road. Alg said that he had saved my life and that I was now indebted to him.

We got to the country club and had a briefing. We were shown on a map the booths where we were to deliver our monitors. We drove to the polo fields where the monitors were waiting. Because of the violence, they were afraid to be seen until the last moment. When we arrived with our vehicles, we called out the booth numbers that our monitors were to look after. We handled three booths. We called out the numbers and two groups of monitors came forward. The third group eventually came forward, but they could hardly walk. They had been assaulted by wovits during the night. We asked them if they wanted to go to the hospital but they said they were afraid to and would continue with their monitoring duties.

All three booths were on farms that had been invaded by wovits and the farmers thrown off. It was a tactic of Mugabe to put booths in areas hostile to the opposition. As we approached the first of the booths, the monitors who had been beaten up, started making a racket in the back of the truck. They wanted to talk. They asked us to take them to another farm to see someone. The other farm still had the farmer on it and they wanted to talk to a senior opposition member who lived there. We drove there and they were gone a while. When they returned it was obvious that they were afraid to go to the booth. We talked and in the end it was agreed that they would walk to the booth in the morning while it was still dark so they wouldn't be assaulted on the way there.

The next polling station was a farm that had belonged to a cattle farmer. There were wovits and youth brigade members hanging all around it. The monitors were nervous but nonetheless got out and set themselves up. The third booth was similar, but the monitors for this station didn't seem at all worried. They leapt out of the truck and very happily set up.

The next morning was the first day of voting and we were back at the stations to check in with the monitors. The group who had been beaten up were, to our surprise, in place, even though they had received another beating in the night. They no longer looked scared, but had a real look of determination. The second group were doing well and the third group was as relaxed as ever.

The voting was over three days. At the end of the last day, we took the sheets with the voting figures back to the command post where the data was sent to the capital. It was entered into a database and then emailed out of the country for security reasons. Two of the farmers were chased in their vehicle by CIO agents armed with AK47s. The chase went on for some time and we were able to keep in touch with them over our farm radios. They managed to lose the CIO. They were probably chased to allow for some rigging to take place.

On the second day, we realized why the monitors at the third booth were so relaxed. They were working for the CIO and had been deliberately falsifying the data. Alg and I made note of this and recorded it.

At the end of voting, we followed the boxes to the place where the counting was to take place. The box from the third booth was picked up by a government vehicle that led us on a merry chase. We managed to stick with it and it pulled in at a known Mugabe supporter's house. A crowd of people was blocking our view of the box. We were certain that they were stuffing ballots into the box. We radioed it through to the command post and they recorded that suspicious behavior took place. The other two boxes we managed to follow without incidence. Again the monitors who had been beaten twice earlier, received another beating by CIO agents that night.

As we were returning home, we heard that around the country CIO agents were raiding election monitoring command posts and the computers were being confiscated. We received a tip that our post was to be raided and managed to get the computer and data removed before they arrived.

With the voting over, everyone met up for drinks. The atmosphere was upbeat. The ordeal of voting was over and we were convinced that the MDC candidate, Morgan Tsvangarai, was to win a landslide victory. Everywhere people were shouting MDC slogans. The streets were full of people. The feeling was that the end of Mugabe's government was imminent.

The next day we waited for the results to be announced on TV. The cities had voted overwhelmingly for Morgan Tsvangarai. Matabeleland had voted overwhelmingly for Morgan, so had the Eastern Highlands. There was a break in the announcements. When it resumed Mugabe was winning in all the remaining areas. The end result was a victory for Mugabe. The European Union, United States, and Commonwealth declared the election not free and fair. Only a few states with known ties to Mugabe recognized the results. South Africa absurdly said it was not free but fair. We were all in a state of shock. We knew that there was no way ZANU-PF could have won.

Everyone waited for something to happen. The government deployed police and army everywhere. Surely the people would reject the results. Nothing happened. Finally Morgan Tsvangerai made an announcement that the results would be contested in court. Everyone knew that the courts were fully compromised by ZANU-PF. All the judges that were prepared to rule in a nonpartisan manner had been purged from the bench long before. The MDC appeared to have given up. It was apparent that they did not have a plan for dealing with Mugabe's fraudulent win. They had been so sure of victory that they were totally unprepared.

Looking back now, if they had taken a stronger stand and capitalized on the strong feeling of the people, maybe Mugabe could have been toppled. Even more shocking for the farmers, the Commercial Farmers' Union that represents farmers including the people who had been murdered, ran an advert in the State-controlled newspaper congratulating Mugabe on his win. This caused a lot of bad feeling among the farming community.

As much as Morgan Tsvangerai and the MDC appeared to have no plan on how to deal with the theft of the elections, Mugabe and ZANU-PF certainly did have a plan to deal with the MDC. Mugabe was more than ever determined to crush any opposition.

David Wilding-Davies with Richard Clowes
(the coffee consultant that helped us).

Planting coffee.

David Wilding-Davies in the coffee nursery.

Cattle coming home for the evening.

Our first year coffee.

Back patio of our house in 2003.

The bar at the polo crosse club.
(Marty the priest sitting and looking at the camera).

Davey the barman.

Rhoda our maid.

Alan and Aletta.

The gates of Chipinge.

The town of Chipinge.

The "Ashanti Power" soccer team.

Mature coffee.

Father and son, David and Max riding at Ashanti.

Holding the Coffee Grower of the Year Award,
David with Josephat who runs the coffee mill.

△△△
10
▽▽▽

With the elections over, retribution toward all the people who dared stand up to Mugabe was unleashed. Magistrates who had ruled against ZANU-PF members were marched out of their courtrooms and humiliated and beaten. Businesses that had known opposition members working for them were subjected to harassment.

The French government donated Renault tractors to Mugabe's government. These tractors would head out each day from the ZANU-PF offices to plough land on farms that Mugabe had declared would be taken from their owners. They would plough in a haphazard manner, their main intent to disrupt farming operations. Sometimes they would even plough up crops already planted. They caused huge anger and resentment amongst the farming community. Each evening they would be driven back to the District Administrator's office and parked in a locked compound.

One night they all burnt. The ZANU-PF crowd was convinced it was sabotage by the farmers. The police arrested Buster and threw him in prison. It was doubtful it was sabotage and certainly Buster had nothing to do with it. However, Buster was to spend a month in jail until he was released through lack of evidence. It was an unpleasant experience for Buster only made tolerable by the support he was given by the other prisoners all of whom were black. A lot of the prisoners had been put into jail because they were political threats to Mugabe. They would sing and encourage each other to keep strong through the ordeal of being unfairly incarcerated.

After his release, Buster would go to the prison to take food to the inmates and help them get messages to their loved ones.

In Chipinge, our agricultural engineering shop, "Chipinge Diesel," had two employees who had been active MDC members. The shop was owned by Dirk and Rose Du Plooy. Dirk had been the last white district administrator for Chipinge. After independence a lot of the white civil service retired or were encouraged to resign to make room for more blacks. Also a lot of the whites felt their chances for promotion would be limited. A lot of Mugabe supporters with very little education were given senior posts as rewards for their contribution to the liberation struggle. Dirk had resigned and set up Chipinge Diesel. Chipinge Diesel was a filling station, spares shop, repair shop and engineering shop. The lathe operator was very involved with the campaigning and a lady who did the administration was involved with fundraising. The lathe operator was called Blessing and I used to enjoy chatting with him when I went in to buy spares. He felt passionately that history would soon be made and all the things that were wrong with the Mugabe government would become a thing of the past. He felt he had an obligation to his children and future generations of Zimbabweans to stand up to tyranny.

One day a large group of wovits and youth militia, who had been bused in from another district, came running down the road chanting. They ran to the Magistrate's court and dragged the magistrates out of their courtrooms and beat them. I don't know if they were opposition supporters, but the end result was that it would be unlikely if they would make a judgment against ZANU-PF in the future.

After working over the magistrates, they proceeded to Chipinge

Diesel. Dirk had received warning only a few minutes before they arrived. Some of his workers managed to flee. The rest of them took refuge in the office. Dirk locked the doors and windows and with his wife, son, and workers hid. The mob surrounded the building and started shouting and chanting. Dirk called the police who were not prepared to assist. The mob started to smash in the doors. Being an engineering shop the doors were made out of steel with big locks and burglar bars. The mob was not going to knock the doors in quickly. They were screaming that they were going to rape the women and kill the men. Unable to smash the doors in they began to cut through the locks with a hacksaw. Being an engineering shop there were bolt cutters and cutting torches in the workshop but luckily the mob never thought to use them. The standoff continued with the locks slowly being cut through.

The police finally appeared on the scene. They didn't arrest anyone or disperse the mob. They told Dirk that they would escort him, his family and workers to safety if they would open up the doors. Dirk unlocked the doors and the mob rushed in and grabbed them. The police had left. The Chipinge Diesel people were marched down the road by the mob and taken to the government buildings where the district administrator, CIO, and other government departments were located. They were pushed around and the mob was shouting that they were going to rape Dirk's wife. Our farm manager's daughter also worked at Chipinge Diesel and she was pushed and told she was going to be raped. Dirk's wife was knocked to the ground and knocked unconscious. A wovit began to poke her in the genitals. The men were forced to sit on burnt out tractors and pretend that they were driving them. They had to make engine sounds while the mob laughed.

Quite suddenly it was over. The crowd left. Stunned and dazed, the Chipinge Diesel people staggered home. Blessing was not seen around town for a long time, but he stayed very active in the MDC and years later became a member of parliament. Dirk and his son continued to run the shop. Mrs. Du Plooy spent more time in Harare and found it difficult to live in Chipinge. The head of CIO would visit the shop and would take cigarettes and cokes from the kiosk without paying and various perpetrators of the violence would drop in and make veiled threats.

We tried to go back to Canada every year to keep up with our families. We were becoming more and more Zimbabwean, but we wanted to keep our Canadian connections. While we were gone, Pete Human would look after our farm for us. Pete was the biggest man I have ever seen. Big in every way – height, weight and personality. He lived next door to us on a farm with his father. They were Afrikaans, descendants of the Dutch and French settlers who arrived in the Cape in what was to be known as South Africa in the 1500s.

The Afrikaners had been in Africa so long that they called themselves Africans and had developed their own language. In Afrikaans, when addressing a person twenty years or older than you, you address them as either uncle or aunt; Oom or Tante. Pete's father was Oom Jan. The Africans however, called him Chiranga. Everyone had an African name although you may live your whole life and not know it. Other times it was well known and passed down the generations. The Humans had been Chiranga, one who scolds, for generations. Usually the Africans put a lot of thought into naming people and the names often well suited the person. Someone might be called Popcorn if they had a quick temper or Bile if they were a bitter person. Sometimes a name went with a farm. The retired British army Major was called *Chimunyasa*, the one who comes from Nyasaland. The original farmer on his farm had come from Nyasaland, as Malawi was known in colonial times. From then on, every farmer on that land was *Chimunyasa*.

The Africans themselves tended to have Old Testament names, like Misheck or Phineas or Zackaria. Very few had traditional African first names. Some had names that were made from English words. A lot had the suffix '-more': Edmore, Givemore, Trymore, Lovemore, Happymore. Another popular suffix was '-well': Godwell, Kisswell. Some names didn't translate as intended: Notwanted, Batman, Rockface, Psychology, and Battleship.

The Humans did not do a lot of farming. They spent most of their days on the veranda drinking tea and cleaning their guns. They had lots of weapons, everything imaginable. Their house was built like a bunker on the side of a hill and old man Chiranga would talk endlessly about his exploits during the bush war. Every so often we would hear gun shots coming from their farm. The Human's ancestors had fought at Blood River in 1838 when a small group of Boer trekkers had defeated a much larger Zulu force. Before the battle, the Boers prayed. They made a convent with God that if they were able to win the battle against such incredible odds that they would take it as God's will that they were to settle this land. They promised God that they would create a Christian society and forever celebrate him. Pete and his dad regretted that they were born almost two hundred years too late and had missed out on the action.

The Human family had been in Chipinge since the first settlers had trekked north from South Africa with their ox carts in the late 1800s. To demarcate his new farm, Pete's great-great-grandfather had ridden as far as he could each day from where he planned to build his house. Before he turned his horse around and headed back he would plant a peg. He did this for four days in each direction and named his farm *Avontuur* which in Afrikaans means adventure. The name had come to him when he was attacked by a leopard in his tent the first night on his new farm.

The biggest challenge to the early settlers had been the lack of labour. Chipinge was an area in which malaria and sleeping sickness existed. The Shangaans had used the area for hunting at certain times of the year, but there was no permanent settlement. The Shangaan chief had granted the settlers permission to farm in the area, but none of his tribesmen were interested in working on the farms, except for only brief stints. The early settlers had the work of developing the farms themselves. Beef cattle farming was the main enterprise. It was not until the population of Zimbabwe had grown significantly in the 1950s that labour-intensive crops, like coffee, began to be grown in Chipinge.

Malaria killed many of the early settlers. One of our fellow coffee farmers, Tommy Herselman, told us the story of how his great-grandfather survived the disease. Neighbours had not seen his family for a number of weeks, so some rode over to the homestead. They found the whole family dead from malaria, except for the baby, Tommy's grandfather, who somehow had been unaffected by the disease. The parents had died first and the older siblings had looked after the baby until they too had succumbed. The rescued baby was raised by the neighbours and, when he was old enough, went back and regained his family's farm.

On the rare occasion when Pete got off the veranda and came to help us, he was sterling. Pete was completely fluent in the native language, Shona, and understood African culture and the ways of the people. Our workers laughed with him and were equally terrified of him. If anyone wasn't working well, Pete would loom menacingly over them. If that didn't improve their attitude, Pete would ask them their name and from which chief's area they were from. Pete would often know either their father or another close relative.

"Your uncle worked for my father and your great-grandfather was a herd boy for my grandfather," Pete would say, taking advantage of the African reverence for their ancestors. "They were hardworking men and Chief Muvahnasiku gave them good areas to grow maize. Why then are you lazy and dishonest? Do you have no respect for your ancestors?"

It was amazing the positive effect this had on the miscreant.

The other great motivational tool Pete used was humour. If one of the workers was getting tired at the end of the day and complaining that Pete was working him too hard, Pete would say that the girls in house fourteen at Junction Gate say that he has plenty of energy after work. House fourteen was where the prostitutes worked. Everyone on Ashanti thoroughly enjoyed Pete and he was the perfect choice to look after the farm while we travelled.

In 2003, we had barely arrived in Canada to start our holiday when trouble started on our land in Africa. The wovits thought it would be a good time to take over Sweet Acres farm. They were not prepared for Boss Chiranga.

Pete was in the farm store after work hours when trucks carrying wovits arrived. They climbed out of the trucks and started a *jambanja*. A jambanja is a coercive tactic, where wovits camp by your house, singing and drumming all night and try to wear you down.

Word got out that the boss was in the store. The store was surrounded and they began to chant and sing. But instead of finding a Canadian of average build, they found 300 lbs of bearded Afrikaner looming in the doorway. The singing stopped. The wovit leader came forward and told Pete that they were taking over the farm. Pete told them to get lost. Pete was uncertain what to do. He had a weapon in the store. Should he grab it? Should he call the police? Should he wait them out?

The wovits also seemed uncertain how to proceed. The leader then, in an attempt to assert his authority and get the crowd worked up again, started to yell at Pete. "You Breetish, you fucking think you fucking know everything, but us wovits we know fuck all!"

Pete couldn't keep a straight face and said he couldn't agree more. All the tension left. He locked up the store and went to the Land Rover and drove home. The wovits, disappointed that the jambanja wasn't having the desired effect, also went home.

By time we arrived back from Canada, things had settled down a bit. Unfortunately, a friend of ours who was a single mother with two small children and who had been living in one of the houses on Sweet Acres, had been forced to move out so a wovit could move in. They had threatened her with death and had been rattling her doors and turning off her electricity in the night. She had become frightened. One never knew how far the wovits would go with their threats.

In other communities, people had been killed. In our area, they were carrying out mutilations of livestock during the night. Farmers would wake up to find their cattle with their legs cut off or wounded with arrows. I think she did the right thing moving out. When it is not your own farm, there is no point putting yourself and your children through the trauma. The chairman of the local wovits moved in and put up sign at the edge of the road declaring his ownership.

We went to the High Court and won an eviction order against him. However, the sheriff and the police refused to enforce it for fear of victimization. The wovit took over the macadamia plantation and locked the gate into the field. Losing the macadamia nuts would be an economic blow to us and we had legal proof that the wovits occupation of the house and the macadamias was illegal.

Danmore wanted to give the sheriff time to serve the eviction on the wovit and get the police to react. I had doubts this would happen. In the end, Jason made our decision.

On the morning that we usually picked nuts, Jason came to work carrying a larger than usual stick. He announced that he was going to pick nuts and no one should be afraid of a little, pox ridden wovit. We went to the macadamia field, Jason held the wire apart, and we all went in. It was a cold, misty morning. As soon as we were close to finishing picking up the nuts, the wovit arrived. He was spewing venom, waving a machete and saying that we were stealing his nuts. Nobody paid him too much attention so he started madly chopping down one of the macadamia trees. Having not got the desired attention he left. We finished picking the nuts and loaded them on the trailer. The tractor drove off to unload them at the coffee factory.

As we were walking back to start our next job, a Land Rover arrived full of police and the wovit, who was now smirking. They said I was charged with theft and would have to come to the police station in town. I duly went in and showed them the High Court Order declaring the wovit's occupation of the house and the macadamia plantation illegal. They said they refused to recognize High Court Rulings that ruled against Mugabe's "land reform" program.

They charged me, fingerprinted me, and told me to return the stolen nuts to the wovit. I said that the nuts were not stolen and that the police should be charging the wovit.

Every two weeks we would pick the nuts and this charade would be repeated. We did manage to get quite a few nuts picked and the police for all their talk about not recognizing the High Court Order were hesitant to take the issue further. In the end the commanding police officer for Chipinge, who I knew on a personal level and was one of the few police who had been in the force for a long time and was at heart a professional policeman, took me aside.

We talked secretly for a while. He said he had been doing his best to keep me out of jail but he was getting pressure from the CIO to incarcerate me. My continued defiance of the wovit was seen as a threat to the government's plan to use the wovits as an extrajudicial force to carry out the government's wishes. The CIO was afraid that it would encourage others to stand up to them.

Much against my wishes I agreed to back off. The policeman himself was being accused of being soft on farmers and by extension a supporter of the opposition. He felt his job would be in jeopardy. We remained friends throughout the troubles and on many occasions he gave me tipoffs. One of our farmers who was a retired policeman and acted as the security liaison between the farmers and the police was also given valuable intelligence from this man.

The opposition movement was completely nonracial. On the whole Zimbabwe was a very nonracial society. The only Zimbabwean who appeared to have a real racial chip on his shoulder was Mugabe. His campaign speeches were full of diatribes against whites, colonialists, and the West. Interestingly, he had a white helicopter pilot fly him around and had a white doctor.

The black population appeared to not be taken in by his vitriol. Districts with a black electorate would happily elect a white candidate to represent them. Our friend and fellow coffee farmer, Roy Bennett, was a great example. Roy had been a tobacco farmer in Mashonaland. He moved to the Eastern Highlands and bought Charleswood Estate. Before buying the farm, Roy had to apply for a "certificate of no present interest". All farms that changed hands after 1980 had to be first offered to the government for resettlement purposes. If the government felt that the farm was not suitable or needed for resettlement, a certificate of no present interest would be issued and the sale could proceed. We had gone through the same process buying Ashanti. Before proceeding with the purchase Roy also went to see the area chief and asked for his approval. They discussed how Roy could help the community. Roy became a very successful coffee farmer and a popular benefactor in his area.

When the MDC formed, Roy became the candidate for Chimanimani and resoundingly beat the ZANU-PF candidate. There were similar examples throughout the country. Mugabe felt threatened by this and increased his campaign of racial hatred. Whites were vilified and blacks that associated with them were automatically labeled as opposition members and sellouts. Being labeled as an opposition supporter was extremely dangerous. If you held a government job you would lose it. You would be beaten up by the wovits or the youth militia. If you had a nongovernmental job your employer would come under huge pressure to dismiss you.

Mugabe's attempts to create racial tension reached absurd levels. Myself and two other white farmers played in a band with two black musicians. We played once a week at our country club. After playing, we would give the black band members a lift home. But after a while, they asked us to drop them off one kilometer away and they would walk the rest of the way home. Then they didn't want a ride home. Finally, they didn't want to play in the band at all. They were too embarrassed to tell us, but we found out the youth militia was assaulting them because they were seen with whites.

On Ashanti, our young and politically active labour force was becoming of interest to Mugabe's secret police, the Central Intelligence Organization (CIO). Such obvious support for the MDC was a threat to ZANU-PF. The CIO felt something would have to be done. The CIO and ZANU-PF would have to break them.

△△△
11
▽▽▽

*O*ur best friends from Canada, Nick and Ali, and their children came to Africa for a visit. Ali had wanted to go to Disneyland but we convinced her that things were not so bad in Zimbabwe and they would be fine if they came out. In hindsight, maybe they should have gone to Disneyland. They arrived and initially, we had a wonderful time. The children rode ponies, we visited friends, and things were idyllic.

Until one evening the farmer who was our security liaison called and said that he had received a tipoff that we were to have trouble on our farm the next day. We were not sure what form the trouble would take but we did not anticipate anything happening until the afternoon. It usually took the wovits the whole morning to gather a mob and get them worked up with beer and ganja. We decided that after lunch, the women and children would leave the farm and go to visit some friends who had a game park. We were having an early lunch on the veranda, when Wilfred the gardener came running and said that there was a sizable mob on its way. Getting the kids into the car quickly was not easy. They drove out and just as they passed the reservoir, the mob appeared. If we'd been a few minutes longer getting everyone into the car, they would not have been able to leave.

Nick and I locked the gates and went into the house. We locked the doors and drew the curtains. We sat in the living room and waited.

We heard the mob arrive at the gate. We went to the kitchen and peeked out the window. There were lots of people. Not sure what to do, we went up to the bedroom and unlocked the gun cabinet. We had a shotgun and my hunting rifle. We got on the farm radio network and reported the situation.

Then we went back down and peeked through the window again. The crowd had grown. We looked at each other and thought there isn't enough ammunition to sort this size of crowd out, not that we wanted to start shooting, even if they did try to come in. We decided that we would be better off out of the situation altogether. So we opened the back door and crept out.

We went across the lawn and climbed over the security fence. Nobody had seen us and it looked as though we were making our escape. My neighbour decided to call me on the radio to see if we were alright. I was carrying the radio on my belt and had the volume on full. His voice came booming over and gave us a huge fright.

Fortunately the mob was singing and our position wasn't given away. We crawled through the bush and then went through my neighbour's cornfield. We arrived at his gate and went into his house. His farm was close enough to ours that we could hear what was going on, but it was far enough away that we felt safe. We had a cup of tea and waited to see what would happen.

As night approached, the crowd dispersed and we went home. There were some fires still burning outside the gate but nobody had gone into the yard. We walked through the farm village and checked on the workers. Like us, they had been caught by surprise and not all of them had got away. The clerk responsible for the keys to the coffee sheds wouldn't hand over the keys to the mob. They had forced him to crawl under the gate to the house. It is a small gap and I don't know how he managed to fit but he was forced to do it several times. He still wouldn't give up where he kept the keys. He had sensibly hidden them, so they took him to the fermentation tanks. They held him under the water but he remained resolute. They gave up on him and instead tried to force Rhoda our maid to give up the keys to the house and gate. She also refused. After this, I kept all the keys so no one would be in a position of being forced to hand them over. The workers were shaken but otherwise their spirits were good.

The next morning, there were crows hanging around the coffee factory. They had come to feed on the sadza that was left from the wovits' jambanja. When things were good on the farm there was always a crested eagle that would hang around. We began to think of him as a good omen and the crows as a bad omen.

The dust settled and by the end of the week it was as though nothing had ever happened. We had planned to go with Nick and his family on a trip around Zimbabwe. Everything was quiet so we decided to go ahead with our plans. Pete Human was to look in on things for us.

We headed out and drove down out of the hills of Chipinge into the lowveld. From our farm which is in a high rainfall, tropical climate we dropped down into drier cattle farming areas. As the road twisted down the hills the climate became more arid. Two big baobab trees stood on either side of the road and were known as the gates of Chipinge. Once we had passed them we were into true lowveld. Veld is Afrikaans for prairie and is pronounced felt.

We then drove through what used to be known as Tribal Trust Lands. Since independence in 1980, the government has called them communal lands in keeping with their communist diction. Most people still called them reserves or Tribal Trust Lands. Once we were into the reserves, the scenery changed. All along the road were little homesteads. Each homestead was made up of three or four thatched huts – each wife would have her own hut – and a kraal for keeping the cattle in at night. The surrounding area was always depleted of trees. The Africans use wood for fuel as well as for construction materials and their needs always outstrip supply. The only trees to survive were fruit bearing trees.

Next to the huts, there would be some fields where corn or millet would be grown. Every African has a rural home. Even if he works in the city, he would probably have a plot in one of the reserves. He would save his money and slowly build a house where he would plan to retire. He may have his parents living there and he may also have a rural wife who would plant his corn and tend to his cattle or goats.

As we drove on we passed stalls where mats were sold. They were made from the fibrous bark of the baobab tree. The trees all had large patches of bark that had been cut out. Sometimes there would be children selling pineapples or the seeds from the baobab tree at the side of the road. If you stopped, the car would be instantly surrounded by children jostling to sell you their wares. After you had made your purchases and drove off, the children who had been unable to make a sale would look forlornly at you as they disappeared in your rearview mirror.

We drove on and passed through the next commercial farming area called Middle Save. This was an irrigated farming area that drew its water from the Save River. Being hot in the lowveld, they could grow two crops a year; corn or soya bean in the summer and wheat or barley in the winter. We then drove through more communal lands and onto the cattle and game ranching areas.

Finally, we entered Gonerezhou National park. Gonerezhou was one of our favorite parks and we always saw great herds of elephants there. Since the park borders on Mozambique and with Mozambique having had thirty years of civil war and lawlessness, the elephants had been heavily poached. This made them rather cheeky and on a few occasions they charged us. We stayed in a beautiful lodge, which overlooked a river. There was also camping in the park. The year before, a group of us had gone on a camping trip. It was organized by a friend who was an avocado grower. Camping African style was quite an experience for us. Camp servants are brought to cook and clean. Generators provide ice for the gin and tonics. Dinner jackets were brought but were not worn due to the heat.

After a couple of days in the park, we drove Nick and family on to Victoria Falls on the other side of the country from our farm. We stayed in the Victoria Falls Hotel, which is a splendid Edwardian hotel looking over the Zambezi gorge. While we were lounging in the lap of luxury, Pete called to tell us there was a mob of ZANU-PF supporters causing havoc on the farm again. I drove through the night and arrived at the Human's farm early the next morning. Pete told me the mob of twenty people had come to the farm the day before. They had rounded up all the people living on Ashanti and had forced them to chant slogans at the gate to the homestead. They had been there for 36 hours and were tired and cold. The mob had assaulted two of the workers and had broken into the farm store and looted it. One cow, five sheep and nineteen chickens had been eaten. Death threats to me were written on the reservoir.

We had been calling the police but had been unable to get a police response. I was unable to get onto the farm to see if everyone was alright. The same problem was occurring on two other farms at the same time.

It often seems amazing that a mob of twenty people can intimidate a labour force of two hundred, but if the workers put up any resistance the wovits would come back with the army and police and really give the workers a hard time. The workers' attitude was to keep a low profile and if they were forced to chant and sing, to do it and hope that the whole thing would pass. Everyone knew this was political and the government was trying to intimidate them so they wouldn't vote for the opposition. Farms that were considered to have a pro MDC labour force were particularly targeted.

I spent the day trying to get the police to do something. A lot of the police wanted to help but were afraid to as they would be labeled as opposition supporters and would lose their jobs. Phone calls were made to Harare to try to get the police command to do something. I called the Canadian embassy and they in turn called the police. No help was forthcoming.

My friend the policeman told me that evening that he would get me into my home. He convinced the mob to move back from my gates and I was able to get into the house. After he left, the mob came back to the gates and banged metal and drums and sang and shouted. In the night a government truck would come bringing them more beer.

I was so tired from the last few days that I slept through most of it. The next morning the powers that be must have thought that they had met their objectives of intimidating people and the mob left my farm and the other two farms that were also having trouble. The workers were shaken and there was a bit of clean up to do but otherwise we had all survived it alright.

Elizabeth, our female foreman and long time ZANU-PF supporter, had been forced to chant slogans and had abuse shouted at her. People questioned her on why she continued to support ZANU-PF. She said the people causing the trouble did not represent the ideals of the liberation struggle. She openly questioned what had happened to those ideals.

Samson our security guard was nowhere to be seen during the jambanja. Danmore had been singled out for particular abuse and Jason refused to shout any slogans until he realized that his intransigence was making things more difficult for the other workers.

At our farmer meetings we tried to analyze why some farms were getting picked for a jambanja. The government secret intelligence service the CIO had cells throughout the district. They had informants on each farm. They knew which people were supporters of the opposition and they knew which farms had active opposition members on it.

I never inquired about people's political affiliations on Ashanti. I didn't know for certain who on our farm were supporters of the opposition and who were supporters of ZANU-PF. Some people were quite vocal about which party they supported but after elections and the recriminations against the MDC a lot of people were uncomfortable talking about politics.

Without doubt though, most people supported the MDC. Everyone was dissatisfied with the Mugabe government.

We were also popular amongst the local people. Amy and I did quite a bit of work helping the local schools, had learnt to speak the native language, had good relations with the local chief and we were generally well liked. The government was afraid of people who had the potential to influence voters.

Our families made it back from Victoria Falls and our visitors returned to Canada. Nick is an extreme sportsman and had a circle of adrenalin junkie friends. He dined out on his tales of leopard crawling through the bush to escape a mob of angry natives for quite awhile. It certainly provided more of an adrenalin rush than skydiving or extreme skiing.

Any thoughts we may have had about having a hard time in the commercial farming areas were certainly put into perspective when Amy next went to Harare. Mugabe had just unleashed operation Murambatsvina. Murambatsvina translates as "remove the filth" in Shona. The filth in question was the urban population who had voted against him, in particular the people living in shantytowns and the people involved in the informal economy. These were the people Mugabe feared most would join forces against him in a popular uprising. Using the pretext that the shantytowns were a haven for criminals and that the informal traders were sabotaging the economy,

Mugabe unleashed the police on them. No warning was given and simultaneously in all the major urban centres, police descended on their victims with bulldozers and sledgehammers. Market stalls were destroyed and the goods the vendors were selling, either seized or destroyed. Carvings and trinkets that had been carefully carved were thrown on fires. Whole neighbourhoods were razed to the ground.

Amy and Sandy, our neighbour, had to go to Harare to get a tractor part. Driving into Harare, they had the feeling that something was wrong. They drove past Mbare market in Harare, normally a bustling market where you could buy just about anything. It was a popular tourist destination and was often mentioned in guidebooks to Zimbabwe. Amy and her friends used to go there to buy clothes. They would spend hours sifting through piles of clothes and chatting with the cheerful women selling them. The clothes would be taken out of a bale clearly labeled "Aid – Not For Resale" and spread out on tables. The influx of aid clothing had led to the demise of Zimbabwe's once vibrant textile industry.

Amy and her friends would find lovely designer labels for just a few dollars. This time, as they drove past the market, the air was full of smoke from the fires of burning goods and destroyed stalls. There were bulldozers, buses, police, youth militia, and absolute mayhem. There were women crying and others sitting dazed amid the rubble. Amy described it as how one would picture a war zone where an enormous bomb had landed and obliterated the property and lives of people. There was a woman sitting with her child in what had been a dwelling. The only remaining thing was a dresser with its drawers open. The woman was rocking her baby and crying. Amy and Sandy quickly drove out of town and went to our friend Carol's house in the northern suburbs. Carol ran a successful riding stable and was the godmother to our Olivia. Not far from Carol's stable was a shantytown called Hatcliffe Extension.

Previously driving by the shantytown I would see people waiting for a bus to take them into work. I was always amazed how clean and well dressed these people were. Even though they lived in very basic shacks, they were determined to be well turned out, shoes polished, and clothes clean and ironed. Even the children playing in the dirt streets were tidy. Without running water or electricity it must have been quite a feat to achieve this.

Now the whole town was a burning mass of rubble. A lot of our friend's grooms and stable hands came from this town and they were distraught. Since I had a pickup truck, Carol asked me if I could help one of her grooms collect the few remaining possessions that he had managed to save.

As we drove there, he described to me how each week he would set aside some of his wages. He would buy a bag of cement, or maybe some bricks, or maybe a door frame. On his days off, he would go and work on building his house. It had taken two years but he had been very close to completing it. It had been his dream to have a real house. When I saw what remained I was shocked at how thoroughly the police had destroyed it. There was not a whole brick left. The roofing had been shattered into unusable pieces. The door and window frames bent and beaten as to be totally beyond repair.

It was hard to imagine how he must have felt and how heartless the people ordering and committing these atrocities were. Looking at him, I kept thinking of Mugabe's Police Commissioner, Augustine Chihuri's statement, "We must clean the country of the crawling mass of maggots bent on destroying the economy."

Apart from some initial outrage from the outside world, Mugabe and his henchmen had crushed the lives of hundreds of thousands of people without any consequences to themselves.

Before returning to the farm, Amy dropped by to see our friends Viv and Graham Hill. Graham ran the University of Zimbabwe and it seemed like ages since we had all gathered at their house for the annual university Christmas party.

Graham looked visibly stressed. He told Amy that the university had become a political hotbed. The teaching staff and the student body were all active members of the MDC. Mugabe had ordered Graham to make the university nonpolitical. Since ZANU-PF had no support at the university it was effectively an order to bar MDC from the university. The students had rioted and the university was easily sealed by the police. The students were beaten. Tear gas was indiscriminately fired. In the chaos, the police threw a student to his death out of a window.

The riots continued and Graham begged with Morgan Tsvangarai to get his supporters out of the university before they demonstrated. The university had been designed to contain riots and the police were inflicting ever more ruthless treatments on the students who had no means of escape.

Graham's cherished university – that had taken in people born in mud huts and turned out doctors and scientists – where he helped to create a wonderful future for Zimbabwe, had become a place of violence and political intolerance. Graham and Viv left Zimbabwe shortly afterward, unable to witness the destruction of their beloved university and country.

12

W e all tried to keep our heads down and get on with our farming. Inflation was getting out of control and inputs like fuel and chemicals were getting harder to find, but we always managed to make a plan and get what we needed. Some aspects of life seemed very normal. We still went to the polocrosse club on Sundays and rode our horses. The school and clinic continued to run. We went to monthly farmers' meetings. Slowly though, we began to lose members of our community. The store managers in town found that their salaries were not keeping up with inflation and they began to emigrate. A lot of the professional class decided to leave. The vet and electrician left. One of the doctors left. In the cities, the exodus of people was even larger with educated young people leaving in large numbers. People were unwilling to live under Mugabe's increasingly repressive and corrupt government. They were giving up hope of a peaceful, democratic change of government. Eventually, a third of the population would leave.

Some of our workers left to go and work in South Africa. Getting to South Africa is an arduous journey. There is the crocodile infested Limpopo River to cross, then the South African border fence to squeeze through, and all the while trying to avoid the border police. Most of the people crossing into South Africa did not have passports and so were crossing illegally into South Africa. Mugabe had made it difficult to get Zimbabwean citizenship for people he believed would vote for the MDC. A lot of farm workers had Malawian ancestry as their forefathers had come to the less populated Zimbabwe to fill a labour void. By taking away their citizenship he could also take away their right to vote. It reached such absurdity that the daughter of Sir Garfield Todd, one of Rhodesia's former prime ministers, was denied citizenship. She became officially stateless.

But the journey to South Africa was worth it. Even though Zimbabweans did the jobs that no one else wanted to do and were often paid less than the official minimum wage, our former Ashanti workers would return well dressed with what seemed like a fortune. They would buy a new bike, clothes, and maybe even have enough money to pay *lobola* (bride price) for a wife.

Our security guard Samson left at this time. Not to South Africa, but to take up a plot on a commercial farm that had been taken over by Mugabe's wovits. Samson was an ambitious person and, after cleaning up the corruption in the Ashanti farm village, he found his work was no more challenging than being a night watchman. He and Danmore were increasingly at loggerheads. They accused each other of doing witchcraft on each other. Danmore suspected him of being a CIO informant.

Samson thought he would apply his energy to farming. Although Mugabe tried to portray the land invasions as desperate peasants in need of land, very few people actually took up his call for free land. To make it more attractive for people to occupy land, Mugabe offered "new farmers" very cheap loans. With inflation running at well over 100% and the interest on these loans at 10% it was virtually money for free. Samson used his position as a "new farmer" to access one of these loans. He used the money not for farm inputs but to buy an old pickup truck and started a taxi service that did very well for him.

As the land invasions continued, food production declined. In the communal lands, the Africans grow enough for themselves and maybe a small surplus to sell. The commercial farming sector grew most of the surplus food. But the ZANU-PF supporters who were resettled on the commercial farms were not producing much food.

These supporters were not resettled because of any farming skills, but because of their political affiliation. They were given a government allowance as long as they stayed on the farms. We all thought that the government was shooting itself in the foot by being responsible for hunger just before an election. But looking back on it now, I think that, if it was not part of Mugabe's plan, he certainly saw an opportunity and used it to his advantage.

When he first ordered people to invade white-owned farms, very few people had any interest in doing it and they had to be forced or bribed into doing it. As the economy started to collapse, more people became unemployed. The unemployment levels rose to 70%. The staple foodstuff, corn flour, became unavailable in stores. Hungry, jobless people had very little option but to try to get a piece of land and try to grow something to eat. People started to voluntarily move onto farms. However, with seed and fertilizers becoming ever harder to find, they were unable to produce enough food.

Soon seven million people were at risk of starvation – more than half of the population. Mugabe used this as an opportunity to further coerce people into supporting ZANU-PF.

It was illegal for anyone but the government to buy grain or import it. This was all done through the government controlled Grain Marketing Board (GMB). The head of the GMB was a retired army officer and soldiers were posted to guard the depots. Farmers had to deliver their harvest to the government silos. Nobody could store grain on their farms or transport anywhere but to the government silos. To buy grain for milling, you had to be a registered miller. The government issued licenses. The government sold grain to the millers at less money than they paid the farmers. The retail price for flour was controlled by the government. The licensed millers could sell the grain back to the GMB and make a profit without even milling it.

Because the retail price was controlled, most of the flour was not sold through official channels but through the black market. The end result was a very powerful political tool. The population was hungry. There was only a limited amount of food and the government of Robert Mugabe had complete control of it. They could deny it to people opposed to them and give it to people they wanted to reward. No wonder Robert Mugabe didn't want to accept food aid from the international community. A group of doctors from Physicians for Human Rights summed it up, "In our opinion, starvation and eventually death will occur along party political lines."

At this time there were still nongovernmental organizations (NGOs) operating in the country. We had great excitement on the farm one day. A truck chartered by the UN to carry food aid had gone off the road. The driver had put the transmission into neutral at the top of the hill where the road went from Ashanti to our neighbour's farm. The truck had gathered enormous speed and the driver was unable to make the corner past the farmhouse. The driver was killed. Our workers said his head had been severed from his body in the impact. The passengers, who he had been illegally transporting on top of the load, were also killed. Bags of flour and tins of oil marked, *Gift from the United States of America*, lay everywhere. The police arrived, but soon gave up trying to stop people from carrying off the food.

The food had been destined to feed the wovits who had invaded a farm further down the road. The farm had once been a productive coffee, corn, and cattle farm. Beneath the state-of-the-art centre pivot irrigation system, a hut had been erected and the irrigation motor stolen. The farm now produced nothing and the "new farmers" were in need of food aid. It didn't seem right and since Canada contributed to the United Nations Food Program I questioned this use of food aid with our embassy. It was explained to me that food aid must go to everyone in need and there must be no bias in its distribution. Our workers were less charitable and said the deaths of the driver and passengers and the destruction of the truck were a consequence of anger from their ancestors and God at the UN and USA for feeding the wovits.

We would see vehicles belonging to various NGOs driving around the roads. They were invariably white, luxury land cruisers with a large antenna resembling a rhino horn on the front. They would be driven by a black man and in the passenger seat would be a Japanese or Nordic passenger. They would hurtle down the roads scattering oxcarts and spraying mud on hapless peasants. They would usually be on their way from an aid project back to their luxury accommodations in the northern suburbs of Harare.

The openings of aid projects were usually an occasion for ZANU-PF officials to try to steal the limelight. The donors would make a speech. Next would be a speech from someone representing ZANU-PF. They would do part of the address in English for the benefit of the donors, and part of the speech in Shona directed more at the audience. Their speech in English would be very different from the Shona one. The NGO representatives would politely smile and nod during the Shona part of the speech not fully understanding the language. Mugabe used the occasion of the opening of a Swedish funded water project to address in Shona his feeling towards whites and members of the MDC, "Those who try to cause disunity among our people must watch out because death will befall them".

For a couple weeks we had a typical NGO vehicle driving around Chipinge. On the side was written, "Christian Care supported by the European Union through the UN." It would drive to farms handing out government "Section 8" eviction notices. Section 8 notices are government bills declaring that the government has acquired the farm for resettlement purposes and it is no longer the property of the farmer. They were often the precursor to the farm being invaded. Again, I questioned this with our embassy and this time the issue was presented to Christian Care and a stop was put to this particular use of their vehicle.

Quite different from the donor community was the Chinese involvement in the country. The Chinese were pouring into Africa with an eye on the continent's abundant resources. They were not concerned about human rights and not in the least perturbed about dealing with ruthless dictators.

Mugabe welcomed them with open arms. After the IMF cut off Zimbabwe and Western governments began applying diplomatic pressure to get Mugabe to respect the rule of law, Mugabe adopted his "look east" policy. He described the Chinese as "the greatest of friends" and readily accepted their soft loans, weapons, and pledge to veto any UN Security Council resolution against him. In return, the Chinese poured into Zimbabwe to plunder resources and take up business opportunities offered to them by Mugabe. Soon there were more Chinese people in Zimbabwe than whites. For all Mugabe's rhetoric about Zimbabwe never again being a colony, it appeared to most Zimbabweans that Mugabe had switched one set of colonial masters for another.

Amy and I had come into Zimbabwe as investors. We went through the Zimbabwe Investment Centre (ZIC). It monitored our project's progress and we had to meet specific goals in job creation, training, and investment. I was chatting with one of the people at ZIC during one of our meetings to report on our project. He told me that they had received a directive from very high up stating that all Chinese projects were to be automatically approved and did not have to meet the usual requirements.

In some ways the Chinese business approach, rather than aid, is probably better for Africa. Investment in business, I believe, has better long-term benefits than straight aid. However, the local population resented their support of Mugabe and their unwillingness to use local labour. When we would see a Chinese road project, the workers were all Chinese, even for the basic labour. Unemployed black men would look on with resentment. The local markets were flooded with cheap Chinese products. The Africans called the Chinese and everything of poor quality *zhing-zhong*.

The anger at the Chinese became apparent when the dock workers in Durban, South Africa refused to unload a Chinese freighter carrying weapons for Zimbabwe. The ship eventually had to leave port and sail to Angola to try to unload the weapons there. Again, the dock workers refused to unload the cargo and the ship was forced to leave port. At sea, the vessel turned off its transponder and there were rumors that the weapons had been transferred to another ship. Eventually the ship turned around and set sail back to China.

South Africa's role as an impartial mediator in the Zimbabwean crisis was questioned when the South African naval vessel, *Drackensburg*, was seen by satellite, refueling the Chinese freighter at sea.

On our farm we began to notice the effects of hunger. The average Zimbabwean, on one dollar a day wage, could afford nothing but the basics, corn flour, cooking oil, and a basic relish. We had a store on our farm where we sold basic items to our farm staff. We got our corn flour from a grinding mill a few kilometres away. It was run by a retired farmer who also kept some pigs that would be fed on the sweepings from the mill. I used to drive down once a week with our two children and, while the flour was being loaded on the truck, we would go see the pigs. We would reach into the pens and scratch the pigs behind their ears.

The retired farmer had his grain allocation reduced and, eventually, he was denied grain by the government controlled grain marketing board. This was because he was selling flour to everyone regardless of his or her political affiliation. Only a few kilometres away in the communal lands, Mugabe had complete control, and unless a ZANU-PF membership card could be produced, flour could not be sold. We were unable to stock flour in our store and the other stores around us also started to run out of corn flour to sell. The work output of the workers started to drop. More workers were absent because they would be off trying to find food. Ashanti is not far from the Mozambique border and corn was readily available to purchase in Mozambique. However, it was illegal for us to import food without a government issued license.

We organized some of our workers to carry the corn over the border at night. They would hide it on a farm on the Zimbabwean side of the border. The next day we would drive our tractor and trailer to the farm and load up the corn. We would then cover the top rows with fertilizer bags and drive back to Ashanti, past a police post and police roadblocks. It appeared as though we were carrying fertilizer.

We also bought black market corn. People with political connections could buy corn fairly easily from the government controlled GMB. They would pay the official price and would sell it at a healthy profit. The people who the government had settled on farms would receive subsidized corn as an inducement to remain as occupiers and we were able to buy some of this corn.

We started to feed all the workers and their children twice a day and sell what we could on a rationed basis through the farm store. Our workers would be inundated by relatives asking for food and they had a difficult time balancing feeding their own families and not upsetting their relatives.

The following year we started to grow our own corn and beans. Worried that the government would confiscate it to feed their supporters, we grew the corn and beans between the coffee rows and shelled it in the coffee factory behind locked gates. We would then store it in three different locations. The workers were all given areas to grow their own crops, which they harvested and stored in their homes. We managed to have no grain taken by the government.

But not everybody in Zimbabwe managed to get enough food. In some of the communal areas, especially ones that supported the MDC, starvation became a problem. Widespread hunger and the stress of living under Mugabe's repressive regime weakened people's immunity and many of our workers who were HIV positive started to develop AIDS.

The HIV infection rate amongst Zimbabweans is one of the highest in the world. Amy and I tried to educate the workers on HIV. We had some excellent drama groups come to the farm and perform HIV awareness plays and Danmore always made sure that there was a big box of condoms available for people to take. We went through a huge amount of condoms. If they were all being used for sex we must have had the most virile workforce imaginable.

I would also try to explain to people how HIV virus is transmitted and how to prevent infection. Often when discussing this, they would look at me with a peculiar look. It was very similar to the look I had when a worker, Joyce, who had a raging infection on her foot from a cut with a hoe, explained to me that the cause was because the wife of a man who liked her had put a curse on her. It was to make her sick so she couldn't steal the man from his wife.

Even amongst our more educated workers there was a lot of denial about AIDS. This went right up to the South African president, Thabo Mbeki, who denied the link between HIV and AIDS. His successor Jacob Zuma claimed that a post coital shower stopped the transmission of the virus and the South African health minister recommended herbal treatments involving beet juice as a cure.

When one of our workers started to lose weight and miss days, we would transfer them to less demanding work. Jobs like being a guard or coffee grader would be less physical and they would start to put on weight and feel stronger. Sadly, antiretroviral drugs were not widely available. When they were, people were often able to make a recovery for up to a year before the symptoms came back. They would then seek the help of a traditional healer. Sometimes they would make a remarkable recovery that would last years, other times they would continue to get sicker.

When an infected worker was close to dying they would come to us and ask to be granted leave to go back to their *musha* or ancestral home. They would often explain that there was an unresolved family matter that needed to be put right before they could feel better again. They would leave very confident that they would return to Ashanti. We knew otherwise and would send them with a meaningful amount of money that we would explain could be taken off future wages. We hoped the money could help provide for the dependents that would be left behind.

Some people who had been at Ashanti for so long that Ashanti had become their *musha* would be buried in the farm cemetery. We would have a coffin built and there was considerable grief. It is particularly sad to have people in the prime of their life die, usually leaving a young family without a parent.

The death rate became so high that skilled jobs like mechanics and tractor drivers had to have assistants. The assistants would in effect be training to do the job and could fill the position if someone passed away.

For some, the abnormal loss of so many young people could only be understood as being caused by witchcraft. This caused further tensions among people as the culprit would be identified, ostracized, and chased from the farm.

Elizabeth, our only female foreman, developed the symptoms of AIDS. Her part-time work as a prostitute put her at high risk. She was very bright and she knew exactly what was killing her. When the time came to return to her musha, she organized her affairs at Ashanti and asked to leave. We arranged for her best friend to go with her as it was a long journey to her home. Her one-year-old child was to stay with one of the other foreman. Her first-born child lived with her mother at her musha and Elizabeth was looking forward to seeing him. Amy got Elizabeth and her friend on the bus and gave Elizabeth money. Amy wished them well and said to Elizabeth that we hoped to see her again soon. Elizabeth looked at Amy and started to cry. She said she knew she would not be coming back.

Our housemaid Rhonda had a brother named Charles, who had gone to South Africa. He had done extremely well in the mines and had risen to the rank of mine captain. During his holidays he would drive home to Zimbabwe and come and visit his sister at Ashanti. There was always great excitement when he arrived. He would drive up in his very nice minibus bringing wonderful gifts for his sister. She had a television and a microwave brought to her one year. That year, he took his sister and her friends to attend an MDC rally in Chimanimani. Both Morgan Tsvangerai and Roy Bennett were addressing the rally and it was a big affair.

Charles was also home to get married. He had lots of girlfriends in South Africa but wanted to marry someone from his own tribe. He found a suitable bride and had no problem paying lobola. He went back to South Africa leaving his new wife in his home in Zimbabwe. Charles would come home as often as he could to visit her and looked forward to the day he would be a father.

Sadly, she started to lose weight and became ill. She died without producing a child. Since he had paid lobola and his wife had not given him a child, his wife's parents were obliged to give Charles one of his deceased wife's sisters. This wife did produce a child, but Charles died of AIDS himself shortly after the little boy was born. Charles's second wife and child became the property of Charles's older brother, who worked on Sweet Acres. The family moved into the brother's house where she became his junior wife.

One of our tractor drivers had three wives die of AIDS and lost all of his children before they were two. One day we were planting seedlings in the small fields on the other side of the river. The fields are very steep on this part of the farm. This particular driver's tractor went over the edge of the field into a steep ravine. It crashed through the jungle and ended up on its side. I remember looking at the tractor and thinking that we would never be able to get it back up the slope. I asked one of the workers where the driver was? He pointed to the edge of the field. The driver was sitting on a rock with a blank stare.

Danmore started to organize people to clear a path to drag the tractor up. I asked how the driver had gone over the edge of the field. The reply was that he was cursed. I spoke to the driver and he said he could not work again until the curse on him was removed. Danmore got the tractor out of the gulley. It is amazing what can be done with a large amount of manpower. The four-wheel drive tractor could not pull it out but forty men could.

Danmore and I discussed what to do with the driver as he had become totally withdrawn and we were afraid that he might become suicidal. We organized a considerable amount of money to pay for a well-respected witchdoctor to remove the curse. I was reluctant at first in case another farm worker would be labeled as the culprit. This turned out not to be the case and the curse was removed. He married for the fourth time and his current wife seems to share his resistance to the HIV virus.

In the evenings, we would listen to the sitrep on the farm radios and respond with "all fine" when Ashanti was called out on the roll call. Afterwards, Amy and I would sit out on the veranda and watch the sun set as we had done every evening since moving to Ashanti. The sun would send its line of darkness up the valley to the top of the hill called Excalibur. Excalibur was now denuded of trees. The wovits had cut them all down and burnt the hillsides. Their small huts dotted the slopes of Excalibur and the soil washed down the hill with the rain, making ugly little scars. The spring that the Afrikaans settlers called *Mooifountain* stopped flowing. And the baboons had moved away – they, too, were looking for better opportunities.

The parrots would still screech into roost in the large mahogany tree in the yard at Ashanti and the cricket and frogs would begin their nocturnal calls. As the sun set, lights from neighbouring farms would begin to flicker in the distance but there were less of them. Our farming community was dying. The drumming would start from the farm villages but it seemed to have lost its happy intensity. There was no music coming from the beer hall at Junction Gate. It had become too dangerous for farm workers to go there. The secret police, the CIO, would abduct and beat them up saying they didn't vote for Mugabe.

Still there was a feeling that things would get better. We would say, " Just as good times don't last forever, neither do bad times." Those of us still farming must keep going and things would improve.

△△△
13
▽▽▽

A year had passed since the flawed presidential elections. We were still farming the best we could and with the addition of the new farm we had doubled the amount of coffee we had planted. We had hired a friend to help with the farming.

Allan Warner had been working one day a week for us to sort out the tractors. I am completely inept when it comes to anything mechanical. Allan and his wife Aletta had been living in one of the homesteads on Sweet Acres for a while and with the increase in our coffee production and my continuing inability to fix anything Allan and Aletta began to work fulltime for us.

Allan was a short, stocky, tough Rhodesian male. The Africans were amazed by his strength. He was hard smoking, hard drinking, hardworking and kindhearted. Aletta, who was a head taller, was dedicated to him and kept smoothing out Allan's rougher edges.

Allan had spent most of his youth as a soldier in the Rhodesian army. He spent sixteen years of his life in the Rhodesian Light Infantry (RLI). The RLI was an elite regiment. During the country's bush war, Allan had seen lots of action and had been involved in some very dangerous covert operations.

Every Zimbabwean home has a bar. When people entertain the

133

men go to the bar and drink. Allan's bar was decorated with all his military memorabilia. There were plaques from various operations, mementos given to Allan by his troopers, the Rhodesian flag, a picture of Ian Smith, etc. Once when Allan was selling a car, the man who came to look at it was a former guerrilla fighter. They had a long, good-natured chat trying to figure out if they had ever shot at each other! We were always amazed how little animosity remained from the bush war in the 1970s. The people of Zimbabwe were getting on with their lives and glad that the war was firmly history.

After Mugabe came to power, Allan and Aletta moved to South Africa. Like a lot of other similar people, they were unsure how they would be received in the new order of things in Zimbabwe. Some Rhodesian servicemen joined the South African security forces but Allan had no desire to fight for the South African system. In the Rhodesian war, Allan felt he was fighting to keep communism and a brutal man from taking over his country.

After living in South Africa for a number of years, Allan and Aletta realized that things were in fact going well in Zimbabwe and there were really no recriminations against former soldiers. They decided to move back to the country of their birth.

To the Africans on Ashanti, no occupation is more prestigious than that of mechanic. Wherever Allan was working there would be half-a-dozen Africans hanging around intently watching. Welding and cutting with a torch were particularly fascinating. Allan would not properly wear his welding mask. He would quickly hold it up to his face just as the welding arc flashed its piercing white light. He would then take the metal over to the grinder and touching it to the spinning wheel, sparks of glowing metal would fly. They would land on his arms and hands but no emotion would register on his face. I constantly had to chase the ever-growing crowd of onlookers out of the workshop.

Allan had four assistants, two from the farm and two assistants that he brought with him. They were the fighter pilot equivalents in the farm worker hierarchy. They smoked the same cigarettes as Allan and couldn't believe their good fortune to be working with a real mechanic. They would hold their cigarettes the same way Allan did; keeping the cigarette between their lips and while they worked ignoring the smoke in their eyes. When the cigarette was down almost to the filter, they would hold it between their thumb and index finger and take one last drag. The cherry would glow red almost touching their fingers and they would then flick it across the workshop yard where it would skid across the stones in a trail of little sparks. Allan's skills weren't only mechanical, he was also an excellent farmer and was a huge help on the farm.

Aletta helped with the farm books and kept check on the dairy cattle. She was very happy on the farm and was delighted that her youngest daughter lived close by and would visit regularly. Aletta was a religious person with a kind and peaceful demeanor. She would often have either a good feeling about something or a bad feeling. Her intuitions were always correct. Aletta referred to the blacks as Kaffirs. I was a bit taken back by it at first until I realized that she meant nothing malicious by it. She would say things like, "Man we have a good bunch of Kaffirs on this farm."

She felt that we were not all the same under the skin and the black and white people thought and behaved very differently. However, she never felt that one was superior to another, only different. When speaking with the farm workers she would expect to call them by their first names and for them to address her as Mrs. Warner or Madame. When speaking in Shona she would use the correct forms of respect for people who in African society would be deserving of respect; older people, people with lots of children, etc.

Unlike in Western society, where old age is something to be pitied; in African society old age is something to be respected and admired.

In a place where the life expectancy is 36 years, old age is unusual. As Aletta said to me, "David just think about it, if one of these guys makes eighty years old, he must have had an amazing combination of good luck, good genetics, incredible health, and made an unusual amount of good decisions resulting in a lot of good circumstances. Who wouldn't respect someone who had all these? It is like one of us becoming a billionaire."

Allan's two assistants that came with them, moved into the cottage next to their house on Sweet Acres. Allan and Aletta were happy to have them living right next door, but would never have considered having them come into their house or socializing with them. Allan and Aletta dealt with any pilfering or dishonest behavior firmly but were never surprised by it and certainly never took it personally.

Aletta would show the utmost kindness to them and would concern herself with their welfare. However, if the problem was caused by witchcraft she would never question it or try to change their attitudes.

The retired British army Major had a different attitude to race. When he moved to Zimbabwe and bought a farm, he was looking forward to helping the native uplift himself; education, morality, and a good work ethic was the key. He was shocked to find that his supervisor had never been inside the homestead. He invited him in and they enjoyed a gin and tonic together. He encouraged everyone to be on a first name basis. He never learnt Shona and encouraged everyone to speak English. He took it personally when his staff was found out to be stealing fertilizer and was shocked when his supervisor and a group of wovits took over a portion of the farm.

After parade in the mornings, when we took roll call and discussed the day's events, I would stop by the workshops to see how Allan was doing. One morning Allan told me that one of his assistants, who had a relative in town, had heard something. It was a tipoff that we would be having more trouble on our farm the next day.

We often received tipoffs. Sometimes they would be accurate, sometimes not. Sometimes they would be part of the intimidation process. You might receive a note telling you not to sleep in your house that night. Maybe it is a genuine tipoff from some one who is concerned; maybe it is a hoax to make you feel nervous. This particular tip came from a reliable person so we took it seriously. We all discussed what we should do, it is always hard to know what the right thing to do is, each time is different.

Sometimes it is best not to be around. If the farmer is the key person they want to intimidate and the farmer is not there, they might lose interest. Sometimes they may want to take over the house but if you are in the house with the doors locked they will be less inclined to break in.

Allan wanted to stay in his house. I thought it best to not be there. In the end we decided that we would leave for the day. There was a school swimming gala taking place in the lowveld. Amy and the children would be going to that. I would go to a friend's farm and monitor the situation from there. Aletta talked Allan out of staying in his house. They would go to Aletta's sister's farm about thirty kilometres away.

I told the labour what I had been told. We decided that they would not go to work and if there was any trouble they would disperse. I went over to Tim Fennel's farm, which is close enough that we could monitor the situation. Usually trouble doesn't start until the afternoon as the thugs need a couple of hours to drink and smoke marijuana and work themselves up.

We had stationed a couple of Tim's workers around my farm to look for anything suspicious and report back. We had a couple of our security guards on a hillside, which gave them a good view of any crowds coming down the road.

By early afternoon nothing had happened. We decided to have a look ourselves. I hid under some blankets in the back of Tim's land cruiser and Tim drove. We went past the farm and everything looked quiet. We drove on to the little town of Junction Gate and turned around. If things were quiet when we went past the farm this time, we would drive in and Tim would pretend that he was looking for me. As we got closer to the farm we could see that things were different. There was smoke coming from the factory and none of the workers were anywhere to be seen. We drove back to Tim's farm. When we got to Tim's farm Tim's father told us that a truck with ZANU-PF officials just left. They were looking for me.

I decided to put a bit more distance between them and myself and drove to the other side of town and met up with my friend from the election monitoring days, Algie Taffs. I was hoping that our Ashanti workers had gotten out of the way in time. I received a phone call from Allan and Aletta. They were with Aletta's sister on her farm. A crowd had gathered outside the gate and was becoming violent.

Over our farm radios we were getting reports that another farm close to ours was having trouble. The farm belonged to Carolyn and Buster. Buster was away in Mozambique and Carolyn and her senile mother were alone in the house. As usual the police were finding all sorts of excuses not to respond to the incidences. The crowd at Aletta's sister's farm had come through the security fence and were banging on the doors and throwing things into the swimming pool. At Carolyn's farm the crowd had also come through the fence and had surrounded the house.

I got reports from my farm that the tractors had been taken and our pickup truck was being used to transport the thugs around the district. I had no word on how the workers were coping. The problems continued through the night.

The next day the mob broke into Carolyn's house. She and her mother had taken refuge in the bedroom upstairs and had barred the door. The mob was trying to smash the door in. Everybody was listening to the farm radios and was on standby to go and assist if the situation became more serious.

Of course the situation already was serious. The reality was no one knew how to respond. In other areas, farmers had gone to each other's aid. In some areas, they had fought the wovits to get to a farmer who was in distress. They were then arrested and charged by the police for assault against the wovits. There was also a feeling that the government was trying to provoke us to react, especially with weapons, which they could use as an excuse to unleash further violence.

Up until now in our district, the policy of waiting out the wovits had worked. After a time, the jambanja would start to run out of steam, the police would make a feeble response, and the wovits would slowly disperse. However, the jambanjas seemed to be increasingly more determined and violent.

The mob at Carolyn's farm had got her truck and had started to throw her furniture on it. They managed to break the door to her bedroom down. She had a canister of pepper spray. When they came in through the door she sprayed them in the face. They ran out of the house screaming. The police came on the third day and reluctantly ordered the people to leave. Of course no one was charged with any crimes.

Allan wasn't faring too much better over at Aletta's sister's farm. Allan had walked out to see what was going on. One of the wovits had become aggressive and Allan had pushed him. When it comes to a fight Allan can't help himself from getting caught up. The police who had been refusing to come out now very quickly came to the farm to charge him with attempted murder. Allan refused to leave the women in the house until the police had removed the mob. The police wouldn't do it, so the standoff continued. The next day, which was the third day of the troubles, the mob left.

On our farm things weren't going too well. The Canadian Embassy had been making some calls on our behalf to the police. They would ask the police if they were aware of what was happening? The police would say they were. The embassy would ask if they had responded. The police would say they had not. The Canadian Embassy would ask why. They would say they had no transport. What if we provide transport? No manpower to go, etc. The idea was that the embassy would make them aware that the Canadian government was concerned for their nationals and hopefully the police would respond. I don't think the police gave a toss because inevitably they would come to our farm last.

On the evening of the third day, I managed to get the police to escort me back to the house. The police had moved the mob back from my gates and from the gates to Allan's house. By the time I was in our house, it was dark outside. I called Allan who by now was out of Alettas's sister's farm. I told him it was okay for him to return to their house. He drove in and found the mob back at his gate. He turned around and drove to my house where he found the mob back at my gate. He drove out and made plans to go in later in the evening. At 2:00 in the morning, dressed in black, he had his daughter drive past the farm. Reliving his old army days, he rolled out of the car and leopard crawled to the security fence. He cut a hole in the fence, crawled across the lawn, and just as he arrived at the veranda saw that the wovits had set up on his veranda. He decided he couldn't get in without waking them so he crawled back out.

During the night the wovits tried to keep me awake but I slept quite well. In the morning when I walked out of the kitchen door I found that they had defecated on the doorstep and had moved my veranda furniture around. I suppose it was to make sure I knew that they could come in through the security fence and past our dogs. On the reservoir tank they had written "Death to Davis" and other threats. At about 9:00 in the morning they left and half an hour later the police arrived, supposedly to enforce the law. It was pretty obvious that the police were working hand in hand with the wovits.

That afternoon, Carolyn and I went to meet with a representative of the International Committee of the Red Cross. They were concerned about what was happening and had come to Chipinge on a fact-finding mission. Their mode of operation required that they remain completely neutral. To see us they had to get permission from the relevant government authorities. Over the next three years, we stayed in contact with them and tried to keep them informed on what was happening. However, when the situation was serious in Chipinge, they were unable to get visitor permission from either the governor or the district administrator.

Over the next month, the wovits kept up a campaign of writing death threats and ZANU-PF slogans on walls of the reservoirs on the farm. I would send someone out to whitewash over the writing. The MDC supporters would then come and write threats to the wovits and MDC slogans on the walls. The end result was I had the best whitewashed walls in the entire district.

One night, some of my workers were woken by a group of women they did not know. They said that their friend, who was very pregnant, had collapsed in a waterway in one of our fields and pleaded for help. Three of our workers went back with the women to help. When they got to the waterway they found the apparently pregnant woman covered with cardboard. But the cardboard was thrown off to reveal a man. Other men came out of the coffee and proceeded to beat the workers. One managed to get away and raise the alarm. Other Ashanti people came to their aid and the assailants ran away.

In the morning, we found a note saying that I was to be next. The workers who had been assaulted refused to go to the police the next day. I couldn't blame them. The police wouldn't do a thing since it was political intimidation. If anything they would twist it and try to charge the workers with some crime. A lot of crimes were never reported to the police.

I started to be more cautious when I went out at night. I would carry a revolver, radio, and bear spray. Nick, who had been caught in a jamabanja while visiting from Canada, had sent me bear spray. Bear spray is pepper spray that is used to repel a bear attack. It comes in a canister the size of a small fire extinguisher. After seeing how the small canister of pepper spray worked so well for Carolyn, I felt very confident with the magnum sized one. Often the shepherd would come to get me at night if one of the ewes was having trouble lambing. The sheepfold was about a kilometer from our house. I worried I might be attacked when I went out. Luckily I never was. My workers were very good at judging the situation and on a couple of occasions warned me not to go out at night.

At this time we had an excellent Canadian Ambassador in Jim Wall. Since Zimbabwe had been kicked out of the Commonwealth we no longer had a High Commissioner, instead an ambassador represented Canada. Jim had become legendary in Zimbabwe. At one point the wovits were going to businesses in Harare and forcing them to handover money. Often they would claim to be representing disgruntled workers and would claim that the employees were owed money. This enabled the government to claim that they were a party of the workers looking out for their interests. In reality, the government was enabling their wovits to finance themselves.

On one occasion the wovits claimed that the United Nations owed some of their Zimbabwean employees money. A Canadian who was working in the U.N. was targeted and threatened. When he refused to give the wovits money, he was shoved into a car and abducted. He managed to get hold of Jim on his cellphone. Jim managed to follow the car to the ZANU-PF headquarters. Jim got into the room where the Canadian was being held and after a bit of a scuffle managed to get him out. That incident did wonders for the Canadians in the country. I would be in a bar and some one would hear my accent and when they found out I was from Canada, the person would say, "You'll be alright here. You've got Jim Wall." People would buy me drinks and talk about Mounties, Jim Wall, and other Canadian icons.

As another form of harassment, the government would claim that all commercial agricultural properties had become state property and they would have to do evaluations of the farms. The legality of the whole thing was debatable. The evaluation team would be made up of army, police, CIO, wovits, and local politicians and they would be armed with automatic weapons. They would walk around the farm buildings, count the tractors, and look for stored grain. They then would come into the house and poke through everything. The searches had nothing to do with valuations and everything to do with harassment. Most people decided it was best just to let them do it.

When the retired British Major allowed them into his home to carry out the evaluation, the wovits were armed with an AK47, which they shoved up his wife's nose. It must have taken all of the Major's self-control not to react.

Amy and I felt strongly that we would not let them into our house. They could do evaluations outside but not on our personal property. One day I was in Mutare at a Coffee Mill meeting. When I got home, Amy told me that a large group of army, police, war veterans, CIO, and general thugs had come to the house. They were aggressive and abusive. They wanted to enter our house to do an evaluation. Amy kept the gate locked and refused to let them in. They threatened to throw us off our farm and to sort us out. They said they would be back the next day.

The following day, we were in our house when we heard vehicles arriving. We locked the doors and drew the curtains. Neither of us wanted to see them and we felt nothing useful would come from talking to them. We hoped that if they saw no one they would assume nobody was at home and would leave. We had hidden the car around the back of the garage and had a means of looking out through the pantry window. We could see the gate but it was hard for anyone to see us. The vehicles stopped at the gate and honked their horns. When no one came out they started to ram the gate. The gate bent but didn't break. They turned around and left. We radioed over to our neighbours and told them to be alert.

Our neighbor Sandy was on the farm with her elderly father-in-law. Her husband was away. She ran down her laneway to lock the gates but got there too late. The convoy of vehicles had arrived and had gotten through. They were armed and very aggressive. They were led by a man named Joseph Chiminya. He was the commander of the CIO for Chipinge district. We would have a lot to do with him over the next few years. He threatened that they would gang rape her. When Sandy's eighty-year-old father-in-law tried to protect her, he was roughly handled.

Sandy had the presence of mind to call a friend on her cellphone. The friend could hear what was going on without the mob knowing it. The friend was able to keep us informed so that if things became worse someone could try to respond. The mob harassed Sandy and her father-in-law for forty-five minutes, then walked around and did their evaluation. When they left, they asked Sandy to get a message to me that they would be back to my farm again that day.

At the school we were having a sports day so Amy and I went there to watch the children and to be out of the way of thugs. The wovits went to two other farms that day. We were picking coffee on the farm and I would have to return that afternoon to unlock the workshop to get the tractors out. I had left the keys in the house. We decided that I would go back with a friend in his truck since they would be looking for my vehicle. We would drive back and if things looked quiet, I would get the keys from the house and go to unlock the workshop.

We drove down the road with me crouched down in the passenger seat. As we pulled up at the gates, I remembered that I left the keys to the house with Amy at the school. We turned around and drove out and went back to the school. We got the keys and drove back again to our farm. As we approached the farm, I saw two vehicles with armed ZANU-PF thugs coming towards us. I ducked down in the passenger seat before they could have seen me. They approached and when they were about fifty metres in front of us they swung their vehicles to block the road. My friend had to stop as he could not get around or turn around in time. They knew I was in the vehicle.

They came over to our vehicle and took me out of the truck. I was put in the back of their truck and had a youth who looked about fourteen wearing a tattered police uniform point an AK47 at me. They drove me off and prevented my friend from following. We went down the tar road and then turned off suddenly onto a dirt road.

My friend had no idea where I was taken to and went back to the school to report that I had been abducted. I was driven a short distance when we stopped outside a farm store. They were abusive and threatening. I had learnt that the best thing was to keep quiet and focus on the leader who was Joseph Chiminya. I kept eye contact with him and tried to ignore the other wovits who were getting progressively more aggressive. I was unsure whether they were going to carry out their threats to beat me or worse. After haranguing me for a while, I was driven back to our farm. They demanded that I open my gates and my house to them. I refused. Luckily I had given the keys to my friend before going with them so even if I gave in I still couldn't open things for them.

After a while, they could see that I was not getting rattled and they said they were going to leave. I said since they had abducted me they had better take me back to the school where my vehicle was. Without any malice, they said of course, and drove me to the school. As we drove down the road, there were people stationed every few kilometres. They would do the ZANU-PF salute as we passed. They were the Majibas or lookouts. This was how they knew I was in my friend's vehicle when they abducted me. It gave me a good chance to see who was being used as an informant in our area. In the future, if I saw these people on the road I knew that trouble was brewing. When I got back to the school everyone was very relieved to see me.

Things settled down and months passed without any further incidents. We had postponed our annual trip to Canada and now decided that it would be a good time to go.

While we were in Canada visiting family, Allan called to say that a large delegation including police, army, CIO, and wovits had come to the farm telling him that they were taking over Ashanti Farm. The group was lead by Joseph Chiminya of the CIO. He said the farm now belonged to him and he was taking possession.

Allan said they did not appear interested in Sweet Acres. He told them we were the legal owners of Ashanti and that he would continue to run the farm for us. Only if the court produced a legal order of eviction would he stop running the farm. They returned on a couple more occasions and each time they were more aggressive in their demands. They drove six head of cattle into the horse paddock next to our house and moved two "guards" into Rhoda's house. Rhoda had a three-room house and now had to share with these people. The "guards" were graduates of Mugabe's notorious youth camps.

The workers were being threatened and Allan was told that we would not be allowed back in our house. We arrived back from Canada and drove to the farm in the late afternoon. We went straight to Allan's house and got a briefing from him. He said the situation was getting tense and they had posted guards at our house. It was the start of the rains and as we were speaking a tropical downpour started. This was a good opportunity to get into the house as the guards would have run for shelter. We got into the car and drove the two kilometres to our house. Sure enough, the guards were nowhere to be seen and we got into the house without a problem. As always it was wonderful to be home, to see the animals and greet the staff. The staff was upset with what had been happening and I assured them we would sort it out.

That night when we were having supper, the CIO drove up to the gate and started honking the horn and shouting. We had the curtains drawn and the doors locked. We went into the pantry and climbed on a chair to peek out at the gate. We could see Joseph Chiminya outside the truck and he looked armed. They drove away and later we went to bed.

There had been a very nasty incident in the neighbouring district that had got us all upset. We had started to take a lot more security measures. I slept with a shotgun next to me. Amy had a .38 Smith & Wesson Special. We set up motion sensor alarms – one on the veranda roof if anyone tried to get to the bedrooms from there and one on the stairs leading to the bedrooms. We had a radio charged and turned on as well as a cellphone and there were two cans of pepper spray next to us. I made sure that, as I was falling asleep, I was primed to deal with anyone who might try to harm us.

The "guards" at Rhoda's house had backed off once I was around. They were still living in Rhoda's house but were keeping a lower profile. I told them that they were not wanted and had better stay out of our way. I started the process of trying to get the police to remove them and to get Joseph to stop harassing us. Legally, we were the owners of the farm and we had a legal right to occupy the farm without interference. The problem was the President.

Mugabe was making public statements that farmers and their workers were enemies of the state and were to be driven from their homes. The police were afraid to enforce the law and the wovits and party supporters were getting away with whatever they wanted. Joseph Chiminya, as head of the CIO for our district, had enormous powers to intimidate.

I was tempted to forcefully evict the guards and drive the cattle out of the paddock. I was advised by my friends to not do it as it could escalate the situation and I could be arrested on some trumped-up charge. It would be better to try to stand my ground and try to get the law to work.

Almost every night we would be subjected to some form of intimidation. Usually it was a vehicle that would drive up in the night full of drunk and armed wovits. They would make noise, bang on the gate and leave. Sometimes Joseph would jam my farm radio so I could not use it. One evening they lit our workers' houses on fire. The houses had thatched roofs and very quickly burned. They had waited until our workers were attending an evening church service and the parents had left their children alone in their homes. It was only through the quick action of our security guards and our neighbours that we were able to get the children out and prevent more houses from being burnt. The ones that were on fire quickly burnt to the ground.

All these incidences were reported to the police. I was not getting much help from them. I would sometimes, after a lot of persuasion, get a policeman to take a statement. Most times I wouldn't even get that far and would be told by the police that the farm now belonged to Joseph as he was a wovit.

One night when Amy had gone to the book club at the school and I was at home with Max and Olivia, I was just getting ready to put the children to bed when Joseph's truck drove up to the gate. Olivia ran to the kitchen window and drew back the curtains to have a look. I yelled at her to stop, but was too late. I could hear the wovits shouting. I took the children upstairs and put them into our bed. I had both weapons out and loaded and sat with them and waited for the wovits to leave.

I think having seen Olivia had encouraged them to make a more determined effort at intimidation because the noise went on a lot longer. There was shouting and the most peculiar music playing. It was as if it was being played at half speed. Our neighbours from next door radioed to see if we were okay. As I was replying, the lights went out. I asked if their power was out as well and they said it wasn't. I thought maybe tonight they would be trying to get into the house. The shouting outside had stopped but the weird music kept playing. I asked if my neighbour could drive over to see what was happening. He said he would work on a plan to get someone over to Ashanti under the guise of responding to the power outage. My radio battery was going to go flat soon so I alerted our security liaison and informed him what was happening and started to try to use the cellphone to get hold of Amy at the school to try to tell her not to come home.

Our landline phone wasn't working. I suspect it had been intentionally disconnected. Everyone I tried didn't answer their phone so I couldn't get a message to her. I decided to use the radio and cellphone sparingly so as not to deplete the batteries. Unaware of the danger, the children were jumping on the bed and diving under the sheets giggling despite my efforts to quiet them so I could hear if the wovits were breaking in.

I had the weapons ready. My neighbour radioed back and said he had contacted a friend, Pierre Nell, who worked for the electrical authority. He would try to come out with some African workers under the pretense of an electrical fault and see what was happening. We waited for what seemed like a long time, but I was much more relaxed knowing someone was coming.

The lights came on and my neighbour radioed to say the electrical authority had arrived and that the electricity had been tampered with at the transformer. Our friend from the electrical authority would drive to my house if it was safe. I responded that the noise had stopped and that I would meet him. He arrived at the gate. I went out to meet him and all seemed quiet. No sign of Joseph and his wovits. He came in and had a cup of tea with me. The children were asleep and a message had got to Amy to not come home until she had received an all clear. Our friend from the electrical authority said that his assistants had been very reluctant to come because they had heard that there was to be big trouble tonight and they were very afraid of Joseph and his wovits. He left and I went to bed.

Not too long after, the lights went out again. At least I had been able to give the phone and radio a short charge. A while later my friend from the electrical authority radioed me to say he was blocked by Joseph's truck as he was trying to leave. Joseph and his gang were extremely drunk and threatening. Joseph was armed with a sub machinegun and in the vehicle he could see an AK47. They had sabotaged the transformer and said they would kill him if he tried to reconnect the power.

He left and drove to the school where he told Amy not to go home. Amy spent the night with our neighbours. At home the weird music started up again and we could hear Joseph and his gang back at the gate. I kept the children in the bed with me and my weapons within reach. In the early hours of the morning, I heard the back door handle turn. It was locked and no one tried to come in further. I don't know what the dogs were doing. They should have barked. It was a long night and I fought to not fall asleep. I was afraid of something happening to the children. In the morning Joseph and his gang had gone and Amy came home.

I called the electrical authority. Pierre had already reported what had happened to his boss at the electrical authority. He didn't want to report it to the police. I asked if I could turn the transformer back on. He said I couldn't as it was a criminal offence for anyone but an employee of the authority to turn it back on. By midday no one had come out. Pierre later told me the workers were all afraid to do it. At lunchtime I had had enough and turned it on.

Before the post-election trouble started, we had very few security measures at our house. The gate to the yard was only a metre plus high and was never locked. Its purpose was to keep the dogs in the yard. We never locked our doors or closed the windows at night. By now, we had raised the gate and locked it and had the doors and windows firmly locked at night.

As an extra precaution I decided to put up a boom to stop any unwanted vehicles from being able to drive down to our house. Next to the coffee factory there was a *gwasha* on one side of the road and a fence on the other. We dug in two posts and fastened another in between with a metal bar through it. We could swing it up and it would stay up because we had a large rock wired onto the end of it. It was well balanced and once it was lowered it would stay down. We had a chain that went around it that could be secured with a padlock. At night and on Sundays we would lock it.

One Sunday, we had Pete Human and his father over for lunch. Pete's sister and her family came as well. They had two children the same age as ours and the children were best of friends.

While everyone was getting settled on the veranda, Pete and I walked out to see the cattle. Like we had so many times in the past, we leaned on the fence to look at the cattle and talk about farming, cattle, and life in general. I said to Pete that the cattle were starting to look thin. Pete responded, "David you are sad and when you are sad your cattle always look thin."

Sunday was typically a day when Joseph would come with his gang to harass us, so we locked the boom in place and locked the gates to the homestead. We were sitting on the veranda at the back of the house having lunch, when we heard a vehicle coming down the lane. There was a tremendous crash followed by shouting.

We snuck around to the edge of the security fence that was covered in bougainvillea and peeked up the laneway. There was Joseph throwing pieces of the boom into the gwasha. He then drove down to the gate and yelled and screamed. We stayed on the veranda and did our best to ignore him. Eventually Joseph left and all of us decided that we would go back to Pete's sister's place for the rest of the afternoon as our nerves were getting frayed at our house.

As we drove down the road we passed the infamous Boss Kloof store. This little farm store had belonged to a farmer but had been taken over by wovits and was a den of iniquity. ZANU-PF used it for a rendezvous point for their thugs.

The man who had taken it over illegally from the owner had a business selling body parts to South Africa. These body parts were sold to witchdoctors. Children had gone missing and it was presumed that this man had abducted them for this trade. Our workers on Ashanti had guards escort the farm children to and from school every day. They were afraid that this man would try to abduct their children. The police supposedly knew what he was doing, but refused to do anything as he was a senior ZANU-PF member.

Parked in the store parking area was a truck with the windshield and front end smashed. Pete said it looked like Joseph's truck. We then realized that what we had seen wasn't him destroying the boom as we had thought, but him moving the wreckage from his truck. He was obviously drunk, as he usually was, and had driven into the boom. Pete and I had a good laugh over it. We decided that we would drive to the police camp and make a report of malicious damage to private property.

We turned around and started to drive to Junction Gate and the police camp. There was a vehicle coming towards us, flashing its lights. We slowed down, but as it approached we could see that there was a very irate Joseph behind the wheel. He swung the vehicle around in an attempt to block the road. I put the pedal to the floor and drove halfway into the ditch and got around. He had borrowed another vehicle at Boss Kloof store and was out for us.

We drove quickly and got away from him. At the police post, the police typically didn't want to take the statement. They said they would have to get the go-ahead from their superiors. Pete had a cellphone and we called to the member-in-charge for the district. He gave them the go-ahead and they took the report. We were surprised but took comfort that some police were prepared to do something.

While this was going on the director from one of the big tea estates was driving his chairman along the Eastern Border Road. The chairman had come from Harare to check on the estate. Unfortunately for him he was wearing a large, wide brimmed hat very similar to the one I always wore. Joseph, still in a rage about driving into our boom, was looking for revenge. He saw the director and his chairman approaching and forced them off the road. He grabbed the chairman and only when he had dragged him out of the vehicle did he realize it was not me.

We all went back to Pete's sister's and had a nice lunch and returned to the farm just before dark. We locked everything and stayed in the house. We heard nothing that night. The next morning I got up at 5:00 as usual, had a cup of coffee and went out the door. When I got to the gate I saw it was unlocked; so was the gate at the factory as well as the doors at the factory. Joseph had come in the night with a locksmith. Nothing was stolen but the intent was to show us that he could get into our buildings. I went and made another police report. It took two hours to convince the police to take the report.

The chairman of our local farmers' association was there to help me. He farmed close to us on the Mozambique border. He had every important phone number imaginable stored in his phone. Whenever he was in a meeting with someone important he would take any opportunity to peek into their Rolodex and get some key phone numbers. He brought up the number for the assistant commissioner of police.

He showed the constable at the desk his cellphone. "Do you see the name next to this number?" The constable nodded.

"Do you recognize the name?" The constable nodded.

"When I press this button the phone will call this person and I will speak to him and tell him that you are refusing to do your duties."

The constable reluctantly picked up his pen and started to take the report. We knew the police would do nothing more than make a report but at least there would be an official record of what had happened. We hoped that one day, when there was a return to the rule of law, people like Joseph Chiminya would be punished.

A week later, three trucks loaded with the usual assortment of army, police, wovits, and general thugs drove around the district telling farmers to vacate their farms. When they were told that they had no legal authority to evict anyone, they replied that they were the law. I had been warned that they were coming and made sure that we were not on the farm that day. Our local farmers' association chairman had received a policy statement from the Reserve Bank in which it stated that there were to be no more illegal evictions of farmers. We were hoping this might be used to get the wovits to stop the harassment.

We drove into the town of Chipinge and went to the Magistrate's Court. We wanted to get an answer from the magistrate as to what was the legal position and why the wovits were ordering farmers to vacate their farms contrary to the policy statement. As we were walking up the steps out of the court, a group of senior police and army officers came out. We knew some of them, but they refused to recognize us.

Inside the court building, we learned that the magistrate had been sent on leave. We found the public prosecutor and he took us into his office. He said the group of policemen we had seen outside, came because they wanted to arrest the farmers for not vacating their farms.

The prosecutor called the Attorney General's office to seek clarification but the Attorney General was out for lunch. The prosecutor said he had a bad feeling about the whole thing and recommended that we keep a low profile.

As we drove away, we decided that it would be best if we all left the district until this thing blew over. We called our wives and told them to pack for the weekend. This was a Friday. Typically if the police were going to put someone in jail without proper reason they did it on a Friday so that the victim would not be able to get a lawyer or a high ranking policeman to order his release, until Monday. We notified the other farmers. Amy was with our farmers' association chairman's wife on their farm and had already packed a bag.

On the way to their farm, we stopped in at the Junction Gate police post to show them the Reserve Bank statement. The police were acting very odd. The sergeant in charge caught my eye and made a sign to be careful. We drove on to the farmers' association president's farm, got the families into the cars and left. We were careful leaving as we suspected the police might have put up a roadblock. We left the district on a dirt road that went past the angling club and encountered no roadblocks.

We drove to Bvumba which is two hours away. It is a picturesque district with lots of mountains and forests. Our farmers' association chairman had a cottage there where we were to make our hideaway. The other farmers stayed in another cottage a few kilometres away.

We all decided to make the most of our exile. Nothing could be done until Monday so we headed off to the famous Leopard Rock Golf Course. We played a round of golf followed by drinks in the bar. Everyone seemed to be able to be jolly and, at least, pretended to have a good time but I had a nasty feeling in the pit of my stomach.

The next morning, Amy and I received word that our gate had been locked and that we had been ordered to vacate our farm. There were "guards" that had been posted to prevent us from entering. We discussed what to do. One option was to drive back on Monday, break the lock off, and enter. The argument against it was that the police would use it as an excuse to arrest me on some trumped-up charge. The other option was to go higher up in the police, to the officer commanding the province, and seek his assistance. Sometimes the police would act responsibly and we thought that might be worth a try.

On Monday all the farmers drove to Mutare, the capital of Manicaland, and had a meeting with the Assistant Commissioner. He listened attentively to our concerns and said he would look into it. I explained my problem and how I had been locked out of my house.

His words were, "As members of the Zimbabwe Republic Police we must never lose sight of the human aspect. You being locked out of your house is inhuman. I will personally call the member-in-charge for Chipinge and instruct him to assist you in returning to your house. You must go to his office tomorrow morning at 9:00 a.m."

It seemed too good to be true. Was the law going to work? The nasty feeling in the pit of my stomach was still there.

The next morning, I went to the police with our security liaison John Burbridge. John had been a senior police officer before going into farming. We were escorted to a room and told to wait. After waiting for a long time, I said to John that I suspected something fishy was brewing. Finally, a policeman came and took us down the hall to the District Administrator's office.

The room was filled with about twenty people representing the army, wovits, land committee, CIO and ZANU-PF party officials. We were told that the farm now belonged to Joseph Chiminya and that they would escort me into the farm so that I could remove my belongings and leave. We tried to explain that this is not what the member-in-charge for Manicaland had said and were then subjected to abuse for about forty-five minutes. I wanted to leave but John recommended we stay. "Let them vent," he said.

At the end of the meeting, the District Administrator said the police would now take me to my farm to move out. I ducked down the hall and out to the parking lot. Jumping into my car, I drove to a store in town that a friend ran. I parked my car around the back and went inside to call the member-in-charge for Manicaland. I explained what had happened and he said he was unable to help me and that I had better do as they say.

The whole thing had been a trap. John being older wasn't so nimble going down the stairs and they had grabbed him and taken him out to the farm. I called my lawyer. I called the farmers' union. I called everyone I could think of. John called me to say he was alright and he was doing his best to stall them. The police and the CIO were calling me telling me to hurry or else there would be consequences for John.

John and I stalled as long as we could while we tried to figure out what to do. My friend Buster came by to keep me company and to help me come up with a plan. We decided I would go back to Ashanti. I would say that we agreed to move out and that a truck was being organized to collect my belongings. We would spin this out as long as we could, then Buster would send his truck and it would have a "breakdown" a few kilometres from the farm. We would continue to stall until we could get John out.

I drove out to the farm. There was a large crowd there being led by a drunk army Major. John was looking quite in control. The major staggered over to his truck to have another drink and John told him that if continued to drink that he would be asked to leave. It was a funny thing to say since they were not letting John leave! Surprisingly, the major seemed to listen.

I sat on the ground and said the truck was on its way. After awhile, the crowd began to get impatient and the feeling was that I should get a tractor and start moving my belongings to the road. I made a call to

Buster and reported back that the truck had left and would be here soon. I waited as long as I dared until the crowd began to get impatient again. I called Buster and reported back to the crowd that the truck had broken down at Denis's farm.

John said to the crowd that it was getting late, everyone was hungry and tired and since Mr. Davies was making an attempt to leave and couldn't, we could continue in the morning. After much secret discussion, the drunk major came back and said the horses had to be moved immediately. I asked for the gate to be unlocked so I could get their halters but Joseph said he would not unlock the gate. I think they were afraid that I might barricade myself in the house and grab a weapon.

John found some rags and I went into the paddock to catch the horses. I caught my horse quite easily but Amy's horse was more difficult. He was always the more flighty of the two. I really didn't want to catch him and move them off the farm. Whenever he let me get close enough to catch him, I would make a noise under my breath to scare him and he would gallop off. Joseph started yelling that I was to take the one I had caught first and come back for the other.

As I went out through the gate the children's pony jumped out. She galloped around sending the wovits flying. People who don't grow up around horses are afraid of them. Understandably so, they are big animals and most Africans have had very little experience with them.

The gate was closed and I started to lead the one horse away. Amy's horse, still in the paddock, started to have huge separation anxiety attacks and was galloping and farting around the paddock. The crowd was looking at him in horror. After I walked 100 metres they started to call for me to bring the horse I was leading back, "Bring the horse back, the one in the paddock is becoming violent," Joseph yelled.

I led my horse back and Amy's horse in the paddock settled down. Seeing that the horses were safely inside the paddock, Joseph started to brag about how in the liberation war he would kill farmers' horses with his automatic weapon. Everybody had had enough for the day and I was forced to promise to have the truck at the farm first thing in the morning.

We spent the night at a neighbour's house and decided that we would try to find a legal solution to this. The problem was that there was no clear law. When the wovits claimed they were the law they really believed it. The President had been telling and letting them get away with whatever they liked for years. Then there was the constitutional law, which protected property rights. To confuse things further there had been a lot of laws passed by the government that were being challenged in the Supreme Court or had not yet been signed into law but which the local police believed to be law. We believed that if we could get an urgent application to chambers in the High Court the judge would have to rule in our favour; that what Joseph was doing was illegal.

Early the next morning we put the children in the car and drove out of Chipinge on the back roads. We arranged with the town doctor to say that we had to rush to Harare as Max had been taken seriously ill. As we were driving the cellphone rang and it was Joseph asking why we were not at the farm. The CIO was always able to get any phone numbers they wanted. We told him our story, which he then confirmed with the doctor. I don't think he believed it but we were out of the district and on our way to Harare.

We got the urgent application to chambers in the High Court and won an order to evict Joseph's "guards", unlock the gate, and bar Joseph from interfering with us now and anytime in the future. It was like a ton of bricks had been lifted from us. Our lawyer did caution us that we were lucky to have had a sympathetic judge and that Joseph and the State would not be giving up. At the same time we were having trouble, another farmer, named Bruce Richter, was having similar problems. His problems were being driven by another CIO commander.

A mutual friend of ours had a friend who worked in the CIO in Harare. Our friend arranged for us to meet with him. His name was Max and he was a high-ranking officer in the organization. He told us that what was happening was not sanctioned by the higher authorities in the organization. He felt that Joseph and the man bothering Bruce were acting without orders and for personal benefit.

Max organized it for us to talk to the Director General of the CIO. We went to the CIO headquarters and were taken to the ninth floor. We were then taken into a room with three men. The Director General was in another room next door. One of the men with us spoke to the Director General over a phone asking us the questions the Director General asked and relayed our answers back to him. We had what seemed like a good meeting and were assured that we should go back to our farms. It is hard to know if the CIO were telling us the truth. They couldn't very well tell us that their local commanders were under instructions to commit illegal activities. However, with court papers in hand and renewed confidence we headed back to Chipinge.

We drove to my workshop and got the bolt cutters. We cut the lock off the gate. Our friend was with us to give us support and made it very clear that it was important to show confidence. We found Danmore who was very relieved and organized with Jason to get everyone back to Ashanti and ready to work. We told them that it was back to work as usual. I found Rhoda and she gave me a big hug. Amy and the children were to stay in Harare until I called to say all was clear. We then drove to Bruce's farm. Mike had organized for a group of other farmers to come over for a get-together. We had a meal, drank some beer and got our spirits up. Our friend had arranged for both Bruce and I to have some farmers stay over at our houses in case there were problems in the night.

The night passed without any problems and the next day I went to get the Sheriff to enforce the High Court Order. He was reluctant and after a week of coaxing and threatening, I was despairing that nothing was going to happen.

Fortunately, we didn't see much of Joseph during this time. We thought he was unsure himself of what to do. But in fact, realizing that he was beaten this time he was organizing a much more sinister plan to get us off our farm.

Eventually, a senior policeman from Chipinge told me that they had been given the go ahead to evict Joseph's guards and remove his cattle. The sheriff came with the police and with much enthusiasm evicted Joseph's guards from the farm. I was at Allan's house and we saw a Land Rover full of armed police chasing Joseph's thugs and cattle down the road. We felt confident that things were turning around.

Rhoda was very relieved to have her house back to herself. The guards had been in a youth camp and were part of Mugabe's youth militia. They told Rhoda stories of committing rapes and acts of violence on people deemed to be enemies of the state. Rhoda was very unsettled to hear youth bragging about such cruelties. She had memories left in her mind from the mid-1980s when, as a young woman, she had witnessed the cruelty of Mugabe's *Gukurahundi* operation.

Gukurnahundi means, "the early rains that wash away the chaff before the spring rains." The chaff Mugabe had in mind was the minority Ndebele tribe who supported his only political rival at that time, Joshua Nkomo and his ZAPU party. Although Mugabe had power at that time he was determined to create a North Korean style, one-party state. Under the pretense of dealing with banditry, Mugabe unleashed his North Korean-trained Fifth Brigade. They massacred thousands of innocent Ndebele leaving a huge emotional scar that has never had a chance to heal. None of the perpetrators has ever been brought to justice. In fact, they have been rewarded for their loyalty to Mugabe. Perence Shiri, the commander of the Fifth Brigade was promoted to Air Marshall and has remained a prominent member of Mugabe's ruling elite.

All of us on Ashanti were hoping that we were not going to have any more trouble. We just wanted to get back to farming, enjoying our families, and having a normal life.

15

*O*ur life did return to normal for a while. Amy and the children came back to the farm and the coffee harvest was going full steam. One day we had 1,000 pickers and brought in 40 tons of cherry. We went back to playing polocrosse and we started to believe that Joseph really had been called off.

In fact, our biggest concern at that time was dealing with inflation that had gone through the stratosphere. It was running at ever-increasing rates; hundreds of percents, thousands of percents, millions of percents – the currency denominations keeping pace, finally culminating in a one hundred trillion dollar note. No calculator, no computer accounting program, no ledger book was set up to handle all the zeros. Store clerks couldn't adjust the prices of store items quickly enough. Restaurants would lose money if patrons lingered before paying their bill. Storekeepers gave up trying to stay ahead of inflation and just didn't restock their stores. Shelves became empty. On Ashanti, no one wanted to work for worthless paper money. Food became the desired form of payment. We were hoping that battling inflation was keeping the wovits fully occupied as well.

Bruce started to get tips that he was going to get more trouble. We called each other on a regular basis and made sure that we were staying confident. He got an anonymous tip that a jambanja was planned for his farm that evening. He decided that he had had enough of running and hiding and that he and his family would rather stick it out on their farm. He was afraid that if he left the house, they might just move in and he would have to get a court order to get them out, a court order that may or may not be enforced.

Bruce locked the gates and waited. At 7:00 in the evening, vehicles filled with wovits started to arrive. Bruce realized that this was a different scene. The wovits were not from our area. They were wearing ZANU-PF t-shirts with the candidate from another area on them and they were carrying bags that they always kept close to them. Bruce suspected that there were weapons inside them. The wovits were being managed by CIO members who would stir them up and then move back out of the scene. Some of the CIO members were armed with AK47s. I spoke to Bruce on the phone. He said they had broken through his security fence and had built a fire on his lawn. They were drinking and drumming. He said he felt okay. His wife and eight-year-old daughter were with him in the house. Bruce tried to call our connection in the CIO who had seemed to have helped us but was unable to get through.

Over the following day as the situation got worse, the people who had been so helpful to us at the CIO were unreachable. It left us wondering who was really speaking the truth. The farmers were all on alert in case the situation got further out of hand. During the night, the crowd got more aggressive. They killed a cow on the lawn and wrote *We will kill you* on the windows with the blood.

A few weeks before another farmer had his prize bull tied up on his lawn and mutilated to death. As usual in these situations, the police refused to assist. The next morning the situation had deteriorated further. Bruce's farm is across from the school. The farmers had gathered there to be ready to go to Bruce's assistance.

Until this occasion, a jambanja would follow a typical pattern.

Usually they would occur on a Wednesday after the local ZANU-PF meeting. Nothing much would happen until after lunch since it would take a few hours to organize a crowd, discuss remuneration, have lunch, get everyone drunk and stoned, and be transported to the farm. The jambanja would typically last until the evening when everyone would go home. Sometimes they would stay during the night if more food and drink could be organized. Eventually, the police would respond before the jambanja lost momentum and things would go back to normal. Our farmers' association would have farmers ready to assist if things got truly out-of-hand, but the perceived wisdom was to let things run their course and peter out. The wovits did not seem to have a lot of conviction in what they were doing.

On Bruce's farm this particular morning, things were not following the usual pattern. The mob was now trying to break down his door. The police had decided to respond and we received confirmation that they had left Chipinge. We had a farmer wait on the road to be able to report to Bruce when they had arrived. The police vehicle appeared but drove right by. On the back of the police Land Rover was a grinding mill. The policeman drove to a farm with squatters and delivered the grinding mill. Obviously the police were not going to help. I wondered why we kept on living in hope that they would.

I called Allan who was still at our farm and asked him to bring the bear spray. Because the phones were compromised, I used the code words, "spicy stuff."

Waiting at the school made us more and more agitated. None of us knew what to do. There was a feeling that the CIO wanted to provoke the farmers into reacting violently, specifically getting us to use a firearm. This would give Mugabe an excuse to increase the violence claiming that there was now an armed-insurrection by farmers. Also, if a large group of farmers appeared, the mob might be more violent than they already were.

Bruce radioed and said they had broken down his door and had entered the house. He then radioed to say that he had taken his family behind an iron bar security screen but the mob was now smashing it down. We then lost radio contact. Deciding that we had better go to his aid, we drove up his lane and to his security fence. There, we met a small group of farmers from a neighbouring district. One of the farmers was the brother of Sharon, Bruce's wife. They had not waited as we had and had already got Bruce and family to safety. One of them went up to the wovits and had distracted them while the others had gone to the back of Bruce's house and had assisted Bruce, Sharon, and their daughter Kimberly to escape through a window. They got them to a vehicle and drove away.

We got back into our vehicles, relieved that Bruce and family were safe, but also feeling unsure that our policy of letting the jambanja run out-of-steam was correct. As we were leaving, the head CIO member drove up and got out his AK47, which he held up for us to see.

We had a meeting at our club that night. Nobody had any idea what to do. There were rumors going around that more farms were going to be attacked in the next week. When we got home we received a message from Pierre Nell who worked for the Electrical Authority. One of his coworkers had heard a rumor that Joseph was going to use the same gang and come to our farm.

We decided that Amy and the children should go to Harare until things settled down. I would stay on the farm, but not sleep in the house. If things got bad on our farm, I would go to Harare and Danmore would help the rest of the Ashanti crew to flee. We still felt that Joseph and his wovits were trying to wear us down by intimidation and the best defense was to not be around.

We had two days of no trouble. We were picking coffee. I was staying at the pulpery until the coffee was pulped and then going to a friend's house for the night. On the third day, one of the tractors broke down. We had been picking coffee in the furthest field and with one less tractor it took a lot longer to weigh and load the cherry. It was dark when I drove up the hill to the pulpery.

As I approached the building, I saw the headlights of a vehicle coming down the lane. Fearing it was Joseph and his gang, I turned the bike around and drove away. From a safe distance, I radioed to Allan but there was no reply. Allan seldom remembered to carry his radio, so I drove to his house where I found him and Aletta at home. They were the ones who had driven down the lane. They had seen me approaching on my bike and then turned around realizing that I was okay. We were all very relieved and decided to have a drink to calm our jumpy nerves before going back to the pulpery.

Allan had just poured the drinks when our neighbour radioed to say that there was quite a noise coming from the pulpery. We feared it might be Joseph and his gang and hoped that the labour had got away in time. Allan and I went over on foot, through the coffee. He got close enough to have a good look. He saw a man with an AK47 at the factory and more vehicles coming. Wovits were busy rounding up the people who had not got away. I went to my friend Tim's house for the night. In the morning, I spoke to my neighbour. He had heard gunshots in the night and heard that they were looking for me. I left for Harare and Alan and Aletta went to Mozambique. Since Allan and Aletta lived on Sweet Acres and the trouble was on Ashanti, we didn't think that they would be troubled but we were not sure. We feared that they may try to use Allan and Aletta to get at me.

Big Pete called to say that he had heard that they had broken down our gate and had broken into our house. Joseph was driving around looking for me, saying that if I didn't remove my belongings and give him the keys, he would start to throw our things out of the house. When I got to Mutare, I phoned the police, but they wouldn't take the report. I got to Harare that evening.

Over the next couple of days, Big Pete Human ran an excellent spy operation. He had his workers go to our farm pretending to be gathering firewood or selling vegetables. They would make contact with our staff and get the messages back to Pete. We were able to put together a picture of what had happened and what was taking place.

Joseph had driven in just after Allan left. Before any of the staff could get away, he rounded them up and held them at gunpoint. His gang then went into the farm village and got everybody out of their houses. They were forced to sit on the ground and were told that Joseph had now taken over the farm and they were going to work for him for free. He shot over their heads to drive the point home. A few of the workers protested and were beaten.

Jason, our senior foreman, refused to be intimidated. He said they were not slaves and would not be forced to work. He was assaulted and his belongings were looted. Jason managed to escape by running into the jungle behind the coffee factory. Joseph sent wovits to look for him, telling the others that Jason was to die. Jason hid in the jungle for four days until he was able to escape to his home district.

The wovits went over to Sweet Acres where they looted our grain and diesel stocks. They took the Sweet Acre tractors from the workshop and, at gunpoint, forced the drivers to move them to Ashanti.

The wovits had moved into our house and were seen walking around in my clothes. They were picking the coffee but had no idea what to do with it. The beans were being piled but not pulped. The pumps had been broken and two of the tractors were damaged.

Meanwhile, Allan got fed up with hiding in Mozambique. He and Aletta came back to Sweet Acres where he could keep the farm running and was able to keep an eye on what was happening at Ashanti. He was not bothered by Joseph, although he was warned that he would be shot if he went on Ashanti.

Amy was very worried about the animals. The horses and cattle were without food and water. We heard that Wilfred our gardener managed to get some water to them and managed to negotiate with the wovits to move them to Sweet Acres farm where they could be cared for. This was good news as animals were often intentionally victimized to get to their owners. The dogs were safe with Rhoda but Amy's cat was still in the house and nobody could get to it to feed it.

We got word that Joseph was organizing a party in our house. He had invited all the local ZANU-PF dignitaries. Rhoda and Loveness, our other maid, were told to come and serve at the party. This would give Rhoda a chance to see if the cat was okay and to try to feed it. When she was in the house she couldn't find the cat or any of the cat food. But then she noticed that Joseph's wife had put the Whiskas dry cat food into dishes and had put them out as hors d'oeuvres The guests were merrily tucking into the cat food.

Outside, the tractors were driven around the yard in some sort of victory parade. One driver drove over the edge of the garden, which had a three-metre retaining wall. They then took off the chains that provided the support for our veranda and used those to pull the tractor back up the wall. Now, the veranda roof was sagging. At the end of the party, Joseph magnanimously told each guest to take something from the house as a gift. People walked out with our stereo, washer, deep freeze and other items.

In Harare, I was not having much luck getting anyone to do anything about our problem. The police were up to their usual evasive behavior refusing to recognize our High Court Order prohibiting Joseph from interfering with us, despite my persistent efforts. I went to the Zimbabwe Investment Centre where we were a registered project that had fulfilled all its obligations with the government. They were sympathetic, but would do nothing.

We were getting ready to go back to the courts with a contempt of court charge against the police. I had a meeting with our CIO connection, Max. He told me to go back to Chipinge and that on Saturday something was going to happen that would enable the police to do something.

I drove back to Chipinge. On the Saturday, the Minister responsible for State Security and Land Reform along with other senior politicians came to Chipinge for a ZANU-PF meeting and addressed the local police, CIO, and district administration. They said that the law must be adhered to and court orders were to be enforced. I found this out from the Rana brothers, friends who ran a bottle store in town. Charlie Rana knew everything that was going on and had an informant who was at the meeting.

The next day, Sunday, I went to the police and showed them my court order. Suddenly they couldn't be more helpful. A team of police lead by Inspector Makota went with me out to our farm. We drove into the yard and I could see piles of coffee still in cherry form. The pump at the factory had been broken and the berries were being pulped.

Our workers were nervous, unsure if the police were here to help us or assist the wovits. When they could, they made signals to me that they were alright. I went with the police to the house. Joseph had billeted his wovits in the stable and garage while Joseph and his wife were living in our house. Joseph wasn't around, but six of his people were. The locks had been changed.

The police started to interview the six people while I went around with two policemen to assess what had been stolen. All our chickens and geese had been eaten as had the children's guinea pigs. There were various items stolen from the yard. We couldn't get into the house and all the curtains were drawn. But we were able to get into the laundry room since one of Joseph's people was sleeping there. Our deep freeze and dryer were missing.

There was a commotion and a truckload of people pulled up. They were CIO. There were words exchanged with the police. Inspector

Makota came up to Allan and me and said it would be best if we went next door to Allan's house on Sweet Acres.

Allan and I drove out and took a detour through the top fields where the workers were picking coffee. We got out of the vehicle and were inundated with people. They were so relieved to see us. They were hugging us, singing, clapping their hands. Some of the old women held our hands and cried. It was a very moving experience. They said they were being badly treated and forced to work without pay. Allan and I told them that things were looking better and that the police were going to help.

At Allan's house, we went into the summer lounge and had a cup of tea. We heard honking at the gate and Joseph's voice screaming, "Warner! Davies!" Outside, we saw the police vehicle and a CIO vehicle at the gate. We were feeling confident so we strode out to the gate. Joseph was beside himself. He was screaming that he was going to kill us. I looked at the police who were standing with their heads down refusing to make eye contact with us. Joseph lunged at me shouting, "I am a killing machine, you will die." He ranted that he had murdered two people in the aftermath of the last election. He had obviously intimidated the police.

With my cellphone, I called the CIO in Harare. I got through to one of the people who had told me to call if there was a problem. He asked to speak to Joseph. I handed the phone to Joseph. He walked away with the phone. He didn't say anything and then put the phone in his pocket and refused to give it back to me. After a while, one of the policemen, a constable, said something and I got my phone back. Joseph yelled a bit more about the farm being his and that Allan and I would be killed if we went back there. They then they all drove off.

I went to Chipinge to see the magistrate. He had presided over the case when the local wovits had looted our store. He had heard the case fairly and the police had testified well against the accused. When the day came to make a ruling, the magistrate was out of town and had left a written ruling. He acquitted the accused. We were deeply disappointed but he later said that he was threatened with severe consequences if he had ruled against the wovits. I went to his office and told him what had gone on. He said, "David, both you and I know what it is like to be the victim of threats and intimidation. We share a common ground. I will see what I can do."

He began to apply a lot of pressure on the sheriff and the police. And I kept up the pressure on the police.

Two days later the police called me in to the station. I didn't know if it was to charge me with some trumped up crime or to help me. In Inspector Makota's office, he told me they were charging Joseph with housebreaking and theft, stock theft, pointing a firearm at a person, shooting a firearm at a person and interfering with a police investigation. They were organizing a detail of police and would be evicting him from the property that day.

I went back to Allan's and we waited. A couple of hours later the police drove past in two vehicles. They were heavily armed. Half an hour later, they came past again chasing Joseph's cattle and wovits down the road. Every so often one of the police would jump out and hit the wovits to make them run faster. The workers at Sweet Acres were celebrating. We went over to Ashanti and received another touching reception.

I felt bad that the workers had to endure such a dehumanizing situation. The stories started to come out. Joseph had locked them into their houses at night so no one could escape. There were always armed men watching over them. Some of the women had been raped and anyone who wasn't obedient to them was beaten. They were taken to parade in the morning where Joseph would carry an AK47.

The police asked me to bring anyone who had been assaulted, shot at, or raped to the police station to give a statement but the women refused to go. I think they were too embarrassed. However the men went in and gave statements. I continued to sleep at Allan's house because we feared that Joseph would attempt to retaliate.

A few nights later, a guard came to Allan's house to say that he saw a vehicle driving down the laneway to our house. Allan and I took our bear spray and went out. We crept through the coffee over to Ashanti. I followed him as he quietly moved closer to the Ashanti factory. We had not brought our radios with us. Aletta back at the house was getting worried as we had been out for a while. She feared that we had been ambushed. She got on the radio and asked for assistance from the other farmers. Allan and I got within sight of the coffee factory and could see nothing out of the ordinary.

We went back to Sweet Acres' coffee factory. The ramp leading to the hopper gives a good vantage point and we had left a vehicle there. The guard at the factory reported that he had seen a vehicle drive into one of the fields. We got in our truck and drove over to look. We went around the field and saw nothing. We went back to the factory. The guard reported more vehicles driving over at Ashanti. We drove out again and saw a vehicle leave Ashanti and head down the road. We thought it must be Joseph's wovits and feeling confident after the fantastic police response the other day, we followed in hot pursuit.

We managed to catch up with the vehicle at Junction Gate where it pulled into the police post. We drove up behind it and got out. We went up to the cab and it turned out to be our neighbours. They had been looking for us after Aletta's radio call. The vehicles we had seen were other farmers looking for us. We were reprimanded for not having our radios with us.

The next morning, one of our workers informed us that there had in fact been an ambush laid for us, but the wovits had been confused with all the vehicles driving around and had abandoned it.

△△△
16
▽▽▽

Work had resumed on the farm. We broke into the house with the help of the police and made an inventory of what had been stolen. My weapons and ammunition had been taken from the gun safe. Every cupboard, drawer, safe and cabinet had been opened and the contents gone. Luckily, Amy had done a good job of taking all our important papers with her. They were trying to find something incriminating. Joseph knew that if he could prove that we were involved with the opposition MDC, he would have the backing of ZANU-PF to take our farm.

Amy and I were not involved with politics, but Joseph was determined to find something. On our bulletin board was a list of overall and gumboot sizes for the workers. They had taken that and had been saying that they had found the MDC membership list.

Rhoda and Loveness, our maids went to work cleaning everything in the house. They were determined to make everything as nice and normal as possible for Amy when she came back.

Allan and I got up one morning to walk to parade. There was a guard at the gate who said that a group of wovits had come in the night. The horses, which were now at Sweet Acres, had been let out onto the road. The guard also said they had gone over to Ashanti and

177

were stealing the coffee. Luckily for us, Joseph had not removed any coffee that we had already processed from the farm. I think he was so confident that we would not get back on the farm that he was in no rush to ship it off. During the three weeks we had been off the farm he had picked some coffee. It would be hurting him that he didn't get any.

Allan and I rushed to the police at Junction Gate. Once again, the police were reluctant to attend the scene. The sergeant in charge had always been useless. He was a recent graduate from the police college and had been promoted because of his loyalty to ZANU-PF. We were getting more and more frustrated. Finally I said that we wanted it recorded that we reported the crime to him and he denied us assistance. We said we were going to deal with it on our own and if anything happened to us or the wovits he would be responsible.

As we were leaving he reluctantly agreed to come with some of his constables. We drove into Ashanti and there were ten people at the factory. One had a wooden replica of an AK47 and the others had bags on them that we suspected carried weapons. We recognized them from Bruce's. Allan and I leapt out of the car and ran towards them. They took off running. We suspected that they had stolen the coffee and we were determined not to let them get away. We rounded them up and marched them into the pulpery.

One of them decided to get aggressive. Allan pulled out his can of bear spray and pointed it at them. They yelled, "He's got chemical" and they backed off.

The police sauntered down to the pulpery and told us to move aside. They would deal with it now. The police spoke to them for some minutes. One by one the thugs walked off with their bags. I am sure they were going to hide their weapons. We told this to the police but they would do nothing. The thugs came and went and we were told by the police to remain in our car. We had called the police at Chipinge and were trying to get a detail up to the farm. The police from Junction

Gate then said they wanted to go back to the post. We told them no way, not until they arrested these people. The sergeant and his constables eventually just walked off.

Once they were gone, the thugs became more aggressive taunting us and singing and drumming. They tried to barricade the road. Allan stormed over and told them to wind their necks in. It started to rain and they went back into the pulpery. Allan and I waited in the car. Hours passed and no police came. The wovits were chanting that they ruled the police and that the police were afraid to arrest them.

Eventually, we left and drove to Chipinge to see if we could get a response from the police. That afternoon they did come out and took the thugs into the post but they released them the next day. I was still sleeping at Allan's and Amy and the children were still in Harare. We were unsure of staying in our house. Another three days passed and we had no other disturbances so we decided to go home.

It was difficult for Amy. We had tried to clean the house and remove any evidence that they had been there, but still it was an awful feeling to know that they had been in the house. I think it was after that day that we knew we had lost our home. We started to lose confidence and we never again felt really safe in our own home.

We wanted to move our important possessions out of the house for safekeeping, but we were afraid of sending the wrong signal to our staff. They were trying so hard to remain resolute and keep their moral up. What would they do if they saw us weakening our resolve?

We decided that we would surreptitiously get our pictures out of the house. The photo albums were easy, but the framed pictures on the walls were more difficult. Most of them were photos taken during our riding days; pictures of us competing in special competitions. When the house staff would go for their lunch break, Amy would cleverly take the pictures off the walls, remove the photos, and replace them with similar pictures she had cut out of magazines. It was quite effective and it was some time before even I noticed that they had been changed.

The cattle were looking thin. I thought about moving them to where there was better grazing.

Our morale might have been flagging, but we had a big coffee crop to get off and hundreds of people that were dependent on us, so work resumed as normal. We organized some parties and killed some sheep for lunch to try to keep everyone's spirits up.

Wilfred the gardener was sent to find Jason who had barely escaped with his life. After a week they both returned and Jason was greeted with huge cheers from the workers. They admired his courage, but we could see that the experience with Joseph had shaken everyone. Amy and I were determined that no one on Ashanti would have to go through this again.

A few months later we were picking coffee in one of the bottom fields. Amy called me on the radio to say the police had called her to say that my firearms had been recovered and that I was to go to the police station in Chipinge to collect them. They were very specific that I was to go at 16:00 hours. By the time I got back to the house and ready to leave it was almost that time. As I drove past the coffee factory I noticed a group of men hanging around. Very often there are people loitering by the factory, sometimes it is relatives of our workers, sometimes vendors coming to sell something, and sometimes performers wanting to put on a drama play.

However, these people didn't look right. I stopped and spoke to them. One of them I recognized as the man who loaded the animal feed into the cars at the farmers' co-op. He had quit his job and become a wovit. They were not very confident and said they were waiting for Joseph to come at 16:00. I drove back to the house and told Amy to come with me. I didn't want her alone if there was going to be trouble. But Amy refused to go anywhere. I had this blind mindset that if the police told you to come at a certain time then you had better do it. Amy, however, saw through the whole thing and recognized that the police were deliberately trying to get me off our farm at a specific time so that Joseph could move back in and take over. Amy had had enough of us ducking and hiding and felt the time had come to make a stand.

Sure enough, at 4:00 p.m. a truck with no front license plates driven by Joseph came in the lane. In the front with him was Mrs. Hungwe, head of the land redistribution committee, and in the back were a group of wovits. Allan had come over and the three of us were waiting at the gate. Amy told us to confront them and that she was not running off to Harare again with the children.

When the truck pulled up I started yelling at them. I told them that they were in violation of a High Court Order. I told them that I would call the Commissioner of Police. On the back of the truck was a policeman. I asked him for his name and the name of the superior who had authorized him to violate the Court Order. I was shouting and pointing my finger.

I went around to the back of the truck to write down the license plate number. Joseph put the vehicle in reverse to prevent me from seeing it. I marched after the truck and they began to reverse at high speeds. The steering became erratic and finally they backed into the coffee and turned around. I was able to see the license plate and wrote it down. The thugs in the back of the truck were ordered by Joseph to get out and Joseph then drove quickly away.

The thugs were a little bewildered and walked down to the factory. They had with them pots and pans, food, and sleeping mats. They said they were staying to guard the property for Joseph. I contacted the police and got the usual runaround. I then called Big Pete Human and some of our other fellow farmers. Within fifteen minutes they had arrived.

We had a discussion on what to do. They were spoiling for a fight. We decided to use the same tactics that they use on us farmers, back on them. We walked up to and surrounded them and told them they had better get off the farm now. They were pushed and shoved a bit to get their attention. They were looking obstinate until Pete, who had been looking at the coffee in the hopper, climbed out. His huge frame threw a shadow over everyone and the thugs took off running. We ran after them yelling. The workers were delighted and yelled at them too. After giving them a good run, we returned to the factory.

Then we realized that we should round up the thugs and take them away from the farm, in case they attempted to come back during the night. We searched the coffee fields for them but didn't find them. We went down the road and found them at Sweet Acres. They had run a surprisingly far distance. The farmer driving told them to get in the back of the truck and he would take them to Chipinge. They said they were afraid to get in the truck because I was in it. They said I could do violence to them. I got out of the truck and asked the driver to drive away and leave me with them. They then very quickly got into the truck and were driven away.

Back at Ashanti, our supervisor Danmore was happy how things had gone. He said that it was time to stand up to the bullying tactics of the wovits. Jason said they were hyenas and were only brave in numbers.

We had peace for two months. Life was quite normal on the farm. We picked coffee. The workers played soccer after work. Drama groups came and did performances. Babies were born. We organized a big soccer tournament between Tim's farm and Ashanti. It was a best of three series. Jason had done an excellent job of coaching the team and had them working much more as a team with passing and planned plays. He also had them do drills and fitness work in the practices. During the tournament Tim and I sat together. Tim organized an umbrella, chairs, and tea. Next to us sat Danmore and Tim's supervisor, Wonder. They had also organized chairs and tea and were staying out of the way of the general audience who were drinking beer, chanting, and dancing.

The tournament was close fought and when a goal was scored

everyone leaped up and cheered. In the end, Tim's team won and big party was thrown for everyone.

By mid-September we had picked about 80% of the coffee. Amy and the children had gone to Canada to visit their grandparents. Then one evening, a vehicle drove up to the gate. It was driven by the District Administrator and in the passenger seat was Joseph Chiminya.

The DA was as obnoxious as ever and said that Joseph was coming to take over the farm the next morning. I told them no way. We were staying. We had the court order.

The next day while I was having breakfast, I heard a vehicle drive up to the coffee factory. Rhoda looked very nervous. I finished my meal and walked up to the factory. There were three wovits sitting on the ground. They had with them cooking pots, sleeping mats, and beer. They said they were the new farm managers for Joseph. I told them to leave and called the police – of course, that was a waste of time. I radioed the farmers who had helped us evict the last group of wovits. Allan was away in South Africa at the time.

When the other farmers arrived, we walked up to the wovits and told them to leave immediately. They refused, so with a can of bear spray, I sprayed the leader who I recognized as being one of the people who had been living in our house back in June. The spray came out of the can with a yellow tracer. I directed it straight into his face and kept spraying. He leaped up bolted away followed by the other wovits. I thought the spray would have left him rolling on the ground in agony and was surprised to see him running away. I took off after him hoping to get close enough to spray him again.

Another farmer ran after the other two waving a stick at them. I managed to get close enough to the leader – he was running very fast – and I let blast with another shot of spray. I got him in the back of the head but, because I was running myself, a portion of spray blew back into my face. It really stung. I don't know how the wovit was able to run like he was with the amount I had sprayed into his face. I could hardly open my eyes and even breathing was difficult.

I staggered back to the coffee factory and washed my eyes with water. The farmer who had chased the other two came back and we went to Chipinge to see his wife who was the community doctor. By the time we got there I was feeling a lot better. She put some drops in my eyes and wrote a statement to say that I had been assaulted. We knew the thugs would try to get the police to arrest us on some trumped up charge like attempted murder which the police would be only too happy to do. We thought we would do our own trumped-up accusation.

We went to the police camp and told them that the thugs had struck me and I had sprayed them in self-defense. I did the usual bit about my High Court Order and that it clearly states that we are not to be interfered with. We drove back to the farm.

As we pulled into the driveway we met the other farmers leaving. They said Joseph had come back and had cocked an automatic weapon at them. They decided to leave. I went back to another farm to give myself some time to figure out what to do next. I spoke with the other farmers and we decided that we would go back and try to chase them off again. We got back to our farm and a group of new thugs had barricaded the road to my house with a makeshift roadblock. They were hanging around looking menacing. I got out of the vehicle and removed the barricade. They were acting threateningly but I felt they would not do anything. We drove down to the house and checked that they had not entered it. We went back to the factory and told the wovits there to start running before we hurt them. They did. We then threw all their belongings in the back of a truck, which we drove to the police post at Junction Gate.

We returned to Ashanti and I was left at home. I hoped we would not have any more trouble. However, I knew in my heart that this was just the start. The next day, Marty our priest came to see me. Marty was always a huge help to everyone in our community. When there was trouble Marty was there to offer guidance and comfort.

Our farm workers were in good spirits. They felt good that we were able to chase the wovits away. We had a week of peace then the District Administrator appeared driving six head of cattle into our horse paddock. He then went to the police and charged us with stock theft. So blatantly corrupt.

Allan got back from South Africa. It was a relief to see him. Allan could always be counted on. We had decided that we would resist any attempts to illegally evict us from our farm and to resist any attempts to harm anyone on our farm. We were bracing ourselves for future trouble. Amy and I sat on the veranda at the end of the day. There was no longer the sitrep to listen to and the roll call had been discontinued. The farmers' association was losing its fighting spirit.

We looked out over the valley that is Ashanti. We watched the darkness march up the opposite side of the valley. The occasional bush fire glowed in the steep valleys as the wovits attempted to clear the last of the riverine forest. The sounds of birds going to roost gave way to the insects of the night. The drumming from the farm villages sounded sadder. The cattle came into the farmyard for the night. I noticed that they looked thin.

As darkness descended, we locked the gate and secured the boom in the laneway. We made sure the children were safe in the house and that our mobile phones and radios were charged and that our flashlights and candles were ready since we often lost power in the night. We made sure we knew where our pepper spray was. We no longer felt secure.

Music no longer came from the beer hall at Junction Gate. Mugabe had banned the gathering of more than four people unless they had police approval. His wovits used any excuse to beat up people.

△△△
17
▽▽▽

I had been in town buying some corn seed and returning home I drove past the coffee factory where I saw a large group of thugs standing around. I stopped and got out of the car and walked up to them. They were a different group. They looked older and more determined. They were armed with sticks and pipes. There were eight of them. I made sure they knew I was not intimidated by them. I went to where the workers were washing coffee. I started working with them. I wanted to give them encouragement and to make sure they knew not to be afraid of the thugs.

Without a lot of help from the other farmers, we would not be able to chase them away. I was reluctant to ask for their help again and didn't want to put anyone at risk. However, the longer the wovits were able to remain on the farm, the more confident they would become. If we were to chase them off we would have to do it that day. The other option would be to try to get the assistance of the police to evict them. That didn't look too promising as the police were certainly going through a very unhelpful phase. The third option was to try to get someone high up in the government to try to get the thugs removed. I decided to go with the third option.

Since it was a Sunday, I would have to get started the next day. The tractors arrived with the coffee from the day's picking in the fields. They waved me over and asked if they should dump the coffee at Ashanti or go over to Sweet Acres and have it pulped there. I said to dump it here as we were not going to let the thugs interfere with our work. I went back to washing the coffee that had been pulped the day before.

Two of the thugs came over to me and wanted to talk. They told me they did not want to be here and were only doing it because they were being forced to. They also said that they were being paid and that the money was needed because their families were starving. I didn't know what to believe but I thought maybe we could get rid of them another way. Maybe I could pay them off.

I tried to keep them engaged in conversation. It was easy as they were very willing to talk. The older one explained that he had worked in the asbestos mines. His name was Elijah. He thought he had a promising career until the mine closed. He had been unable to find work and after a year with no income he had become desperate. The government was offering a work for food program. Elijah signed up for it but found that the work the government had in mind was beating up opponents of ZANU-PF.

Being desperate for the assistance, he unwillingly carried out what was required. He said it was not so bad at first. They would attend ZANU-PF "star rallys" to make the crowds seem bigger. Sometimes at night they would cut the legs off farmers' cattle. Maybe they would burn some farm workers' houses. They would man roadblocks to prevent MDC supporters from attending rallies. Elijah looked down and said, "But they wanted me to do more things. Things I am very ashamed of." They took him away from his home area so he would not be recognized and he was used for "special jobs." He said he could not quit now as he would be jailed for his crimes. He needed the protection of ZANU-PF.

I asked him about the others. He said, "Some are serious but the others are drunkards. They work for drink and mbanje (marijuana). Some are crazy people who the CIO find. We don't like to work with them as their heads are wrong. Sometimes we work with the youth."

The youth are the products of Mugabe's Border Gezi youth camps. Under the auspices of teaching patriotism and as a prerequisite for work in the civil service, youth are taken to the camps. They are taught to hate, torture, and rape.

The other man tapped Elijah on the shoulder. I wondered if Elijah himself was insane as he pointed his finger at me and in a snarling voice spat out, "You British, go home! You stole the land from us. Now we take it back. You think we are fools but we will show you. We will spill blood for Mugabe".

But then I noticed that Joseph had driven in with a truck full of beer and was looking our way.

I decided that later in the evening when everything was quiet, I would come out on my own and tell them that they were not wanted on the farm. I would have a bundle of money to show them and say that I would drive them to the bus station and then give them the money so they could get a bus back to where they came from.

We finished the day's work and the wovits stayed out of our way. I returned to our house and had dinner. I waited until 11:00 that night and then went back out to the factory. They had taken rails from the fence and had a big fire going with them. They also had placed a large log across the laneway. When I arrived at the fire it was obvious that they were drinking and taking drugs. They had some senior CIO members with them who were working them up into a frenzy. The option of trying to pay them to get on a bus and leave wasn't going to work. I walked up to them and demanded that they remove the log that was blocking the road. Surprisingly, they did. I then returned to my house. During the night there was lots of drumming and chanting and vehicles coming and going.

The next morning I went to work as normal. A barricade was set up to prevent the workers from entering the factory area. The workers just walked around it and came to work anyway. I walked up and took the barricade down and told the wovits to wind their necks in. They stayed out of our way and we were able to work unimpeded.

I called my old friend Graham Hill, who had been the Vice Chancellor of the University of Zimbabwe. He knew a lot of the senior ministers in the government as well as Mugabe himself. He had moved to Scotland a few years previously after retiring from the University. Graham said he would be prepared to come out and see if there was anything he could do to help.

Arrangements were made and he was due to fly out in five days time. I placed the call on the cellphone. The phones were certainly compromised but it was supposedly harder for the CIO to monitor cellphones than landlines. We had been told that the Chinese had sold the government equipment to monitor cellphones but they had to be within a certain radius to do it.

A group of elders from Maundwa, a communal land where a lot of our workers came from, arrived at the farm to see me. They were very concerned about the harassment we were having. They said they were praying for us and that God had spoken to them in a dream. In the dream they saw our farm. They said my family and I were safe and happy and that there were flowers blooming. They then instructed me to get water from the farm dam. I was to mix it with salt. I was then to sprinkle the water around the areas where the wovits were hanging out. I was to do this in such a way that they be unaware of what I was doing. This would give me and all the people on the farm protection. It would also harm the thugs if they were to hurt any of us. They said they would continue to pray for us and then they left.

I was determined not to leave the workers in a potentially

dangerous situation. We would hull coffee at night. The hulling process is slow and we worked on two shifts, a regular day shift and another shift that would finish at 10:00 at night. I made sure that I stayed up at the factory until 10:00. I didn't want anything to happen to the workers if I was not there. Joseph would come during that time and would resupply his wovits with booze and drugs. He would get them to chant slogans and dance. He would then yell that he was going to kill me, "Davies you will die. I am a killer. I have killed two people".

I would walk out of the hulling room and up to the fire where he was. "Joseph I am here. If you want to kill me, go ahead and do it or else fuck off."

I would stand with my face inches from his. After some moments he would back off and start singing revolutionary songs. One night, as I was walking back from the factory, I could hear the thugs running down the laneway towards me. I kept walking until they were very close when I turned around. They stopped. I started walking towards them. They backed away and I told them to wind their necks in. I then walked peacefully back to the house.

They were becoming more aggressive but I was becoming less afraid. I think we had been through so much and we had in some ways become resigned to the fact that we could lose the farm. What we would not lose was our dignity. We would not be afraid, we would not abandon our workers and we would not kowtow to these thugs.

The following morning, another delegation, this time from Chidongo which is another communal area, came to see me. They offered their prayers for us and bid us strength in dealing with the wovits. The leader was himself a ZANU-PF supporter. He made it very clear that he did not support what was happening.

The thugs tried to stop Allan from coming to the factory. He had to push his way in with his car. As he was leaving, Wilfred the gardener came to say that the thugs had laid nails on the road. Allan drove out but with one wheel on the middle of the road and one on the edge. The workers were all staying strong and whenever the thugs tried to prevent them from working they would stand their ground.

That evening I was working late hulling coffee with two other workers. We could hear the wovits outside. Some vehicles had arrived and they were working themselves up with booze and chanting. They came running by the hulling room door singing and brandishing chains, pipes, and sticks. Our Jack Russell terriers took off after them nipping at their heels. The three of us had a good laugh. Later, they came back to the door again. The dogs barked and snarled at them. This time, the thugs had sticks with a meter of wire tied on at the end. They swung the wire quickly so that it became invisible and hit the dogs. The dogs were injured and retreated cowering from the pain. I went to the door and told the thugs to fuck off. They left.

I called Allan. He was in town having supper with some friends. I told him things were getting tense and that he had better come back in case I needed backup. We continued working. There was an enormous bang on the roof. It sounded like heavy rocks being thrown onto the roof and clattering down on the tin. We were unaware at the time, but it was automatic weapon fire. They were shooting at the roof. The thugs came back to the door ordering us out. We were not afraid thinking that throwing rocks was not going to scare us. We told them to fuck off. The scene was getting tense. I left the door open to show we were not afraid. They were getting bolder and more aggressive. I felt it was best to go and confront them. I walked out to the fire where they were drinking in between harassing us. I told them to leave us alone, that we would continue to work until 10:00 p.m. They had surrounded me. I had told Allan who was now at his house what I was doing. If I didn't make communications with him by radio or phone within the next few minutes to come over and try to distract them so I could escape or if I was hurt to try to get me out.

I saw the lights of a vehicle coming down the lane. I thought that it was more thugs coming as they were certainly trying to push hard. The vehicle pulled up and to my relief it was Tim Fennel and another farmer. They had had a premonition that I was in trouble and thought they had better come to see if I was alright. The wovits became very agitated. They started to beat the vehicle with sticks and chains. Tim tried to speak to them but they were in no mood for talking. They pushed Tim and his friend and did all sorts of theatrics. I noticed that some of them had gone into the hulling room and had come out dragging the two workers. They were forced to kneel on the ground and chant ZANU-PF slogans. The wovits had a length of fan belt tied to a stick. They beat the workers with it as they chanted the slogans.

As the situation became tenser and the wovits became more focused on us, I saw that the two workers had managed to escape. I tried to walk back to my house but was blocked. Tim suggested that I get in the vehicle and that we would leave. I got in and we drove out.

Another farmer was having a terrible time that night. An elderly couple, Gideon and his wife Leslie, had a group of thugs in their house and were in the process of being evicted violently. We drove to their farm. The police had set up a roadblock and were preventing anyone from going to their aid. We spoke to them on the cellphone. They were much shaken and Leslie was taking it very badly. The person who was taking over their farm was a Zimbabwean diplomat from London. He was smiling and thoroughly enjoying the whole ordeal. There was nothing we could do. The police had cordoned the farm off. It was very upsetting to hear this elderly couple on the farm radio desperately wanting some help and no one able to give them assistance.

We went back to Tim's place for a drink. It was now midnight. We decided that I would go back and spend the night with Allan. I got to Allan's house. Aletta had made some supper for me. We decided that we would do muster parade in the morning at Sweet Acres as usual. We would keep all the workers working on Sweet Acres until Allan and I had a chance to see what the situation was like on Ashanti. We would do a reconnaissance on foot and, if there was no one in our house, I would get inside and at least then I would have possession.

At parade in the morning, the atmosphere was electric. The permanent workers always come to parade, but today, even the pickers who normally go straight to the field had come. So had the women who sell vegetables and other items at the coffee scale. They had sticks and knobkerries and some were wearing hard hats. I told them we would be working at Sweet Acres. They said, "Boss we are going to work at Ashanti. We have a right to work and we are not going to be stopped."

They asked me to lead them in prayer. After praying they sang hymns and then said, "*Endai*, let's go!"

Allan and I looked at each other. Allan had seen a couple of wovits with cellphones watching this whole thing. We decided that maybe this was a make or break it moment, and that if all the workers were up for it, we would give it a go.

I walked through the compound and onto Ashanti. The workers fanned out through the coffee and followed me. Allan came behind pushing his motorbike. We had gone about 300 metres onto Ashanti when Joseph came driving around the corner of the farm road with a truck full of thugs in the back.

The truck skidded to a halt. Joseph leapt out, cocked his 9 mm sub machinegun, and pointed it at Allan's chest and pulled the trigger. In what I will always believe was an act of God, the weapon jammed.

As Joseph worked to clear the blockage, the wovits descended on Allan with pipes. By time I got to him, he was about ten metres from his bike and on the ground. The thugs were on top of him beating him on the head. He was covered with blood and dazed and was trying to defend himself.

As I pulled Allan to his feet, the thugs began hitting me on the back with their pipes. Screaming at them, and with my arm around Allan, we moved off. Allan wanted to go back and fight them. I said no they will kill one of us. Joseph had the weapon unjammed and was firing at us. But, because his thugs were trying to beat us he couldn't lower his weapon to hit us without shooting them. The workers were being scattered by the gunfire. I got Allan to the tar road.

Joseph and his thugs didn't follow us on the road. Big Pete and his dad were driving by. They stopped, shaken to see the state that Allan was in. Allan declined a lift. He wanted to clear his head before getting back to his house and seeing Aletta. When we got to his house, my biggest fear was that Aletta would be distraught at the sight of Allan and I felt guilty because I had got him into this mess. I had always thought that I would be the one getting shot or beaten and Allan would be the one pulling me out of the mess.

I went to Aletta's bedroom. I started to tell her Allan had been hurt but she said she already knew. Aletta was calm. She said she had been praying and knew there was trouble. She knew God was looking over us and would protect us. She checked him over and we got into her car and drove to the clinic. We called ahead to have the doctor ready to meet us.

We were so busy looking at the wounds on Allan's head that we didn't see that his hands were also damaged. Some of the thugs must have been hurting as well.

We couldn't believe that the weapon had jammed. This type of weapon doesn't have a reputation for jamming. People have told us that Joseph had probably never cleaned it and any weapon will jam if it is dirty enough. But, Aletta said she knew that it was an angel that saved him.

At the clinic we met Allan's daughter, Donna. She was shocked to see her dad covered in blood. Marty the priest arrived and was a comfort to everyone.

Petra the doctor, who herself had recently had her hand broken by wovits, felt that the actions of Mugabe and his supporters needed to be recorded. With her digital camera, she took pictures before cleaning and stitching Allan up. She sent these pictures via the internet to various journalists. Within minutes we were getting calls. We told them what had happened.

So often, people in Zimbabwe are afraid to talk to the press in case they are victimized. We had already been victimized. We didn't care about that, but we did care about what was happening in the country. We made a point of telling the reporters that it was not just a case of a white farmer and his family being made homeless and jobless, but also about 250 black families that would be made homeless and jobless.

Petra kept Allan in for a while to observe him. I went to the police where they took my statement. When Allan was discharged we went back for him to make a statement. The police asked me into a room. The three most senior policemen in the district were sitting there. They asked me to take a seat. They were speaking amongst themselves in Shona. I understood and spoke enough Shona to follow the conversation. I don't know whether they thought I didn't understand what they were saying or whether they wanted me to know something without them outwardly saying it.

I heard them say that the senior officer for the province had instructed them to be at Gideon's farm last night and that the senior policeman was to get a piece of that farm. They were under orders to prevent anyone from assisting Gideon and that the CIO and the wovits were to be above the law. They said that all the remaining farmers were to be removed from the area. They also said that they were ashamed of having to operate like this.

The member-in-charge of the district then spoke to me in English We discussed the legal position and I went over the High Court Order with him. He was already familiar with it and said the government had amended the constitution so that the existing order was invalid. I explained that we had gone back to the court and had the order reconfirmed. I also explained to him that it was illegal for anyone to evict someone else without an eviction order, which clearly Joseph didn't have.

After discussing the legal side for a while he said, "We as police have to follow orders. Sometimes we don't agree with these orders but we have to follow them. The people who hold power have declared that white farmers must be removed. By whatever means you, Mr. Davies, will be removed from your farm. Last night Gideon went through an inhuman experience. It was also an inhuman experience for us. Save yourself and everyone from that. Start to move your belongings off your farm. Otherwise you will find yourself in a position where people are running through your house throwing your property on the lawn and you and us can do nothing to stop it."

I thanked him for his advice and left. My biggest concern was the coffee at the factory. We had tens of thousands of dollars worth of coffee in the shed, in the hulling room, and drying on the tables. Without me there the thugs would certainly start to loot. The first thing they would take would be the coffee.

Graham was to arrive the next day. We decided to move our belongings off the farm since that could take a few days, which would give Graham time to see what he could do. That would prevent any looting and if we were able to get back on the farm we would move everything back.

I called the Canadian Embassy. The Ambassador who in the past hadn't been very helpful had left. A new Ambassador, Terry Moonie, had arrived but he hadn't presented his credentials yet. I spoke to him and explained I was planning to move off the farm and would like a representative from the embassy to be there. Terry was to come the following day. I told the police that I would move off on their advice, but I wanted to do it peacefully. I told the farm workers what was happening and that if any of them that wanted to move off too I would help with tractors and accommodate them at Sweet Acres.

Terry arrived the next morning. Terry was born with a disability. His arms end at his elbows and he doesn't have full hands. He is also rather short and balding. We drove up to the farm in the diplomatic vehicle. Terry got out and walked up to the CIO operative that was running the thugs. The thug looked at the deformity. He stared at the fingers that came out of his elbow. He nervously swallowed and shook hands with him.

The thugs melted away. The CIO operative who had been carrying an AK47 went and hid it.

Friends and neighbours brought tractors and trucks to help with the move. As everyone started to pack things up, I was not much help. The whole thing was too emotional for me. I still hoped that Graham could do something, but I was sure that this time the game was up. We had raised our children and enjoyed so much happiness in the house. To think that we were losing it to these thugs was too much. I saw the small details, like where the children were measured against the wall as they grew, and it became too much to handle.

Everyone got the whole house packed and moved by the afternoon. We took off the doors, light fixtures, and even the kitchen cupboards were removed.

The thugs were lounging around. Our workers would bump into them or mutter something nasty to them under their breath whenever they went by. We left the yard and the thugs went into the house to celebrate. All of our workers wanted to leave before nighttime because they were afraid to be left on the farm in the dark. We moved everyone over to Sweet Acres.

Just before dark we started to move the coffee out of the shed. The CIO operative tried to stop us saying that it was now their coffee.

Terry went up to him and pointed his finger and said that we would be removing the coffee, which was our legal right. Once it got dark we left. We would finish the next day.

That night over supper I was saying to Allan what a great job Terry was doing. The thugs seemed to really back off when he was around. Allan said it was because they thought he was a *tikoloshe*. A tikoloshe is a mythical person in African culture. They are short and very strong. They usually do bad things to people.

The next morning, we were back at the farm to get the coffee off. When Allan and I arrived, the thugs were lounging around talking about what a great party they had in our house and the CIO operative was walking around with an AK47 over his shoulder. They said we couldn't take any more coffee off the farm as it was theirs.

Terry arrived, got out of the diplomatic car, pointed his finger at them and things improved. The weapons disappeared. We got the coffee out of the shed and removed it from the drying tables and were ready to drive out of the farm.

Terry called me over. He said he wanted to say something to the CIO operative in charge of the thugs and he wanted me to hear it. His name was Andrew. He called the CIO guy over and began. "On behalf of the Canadian Government and myself I would like to thank you for working with me to enable Mr. Davies to move off peacefully."

I thought I was going to throw up. He continued, "Now Andrew, where we come from, people who are born like this..." holding up his hands, Terry went on, "...have special powers. When I came to this country I went to great Zimbabwe and communed with the spiritual world. I asked for permission to use my powers in this country. That permission was granted to me because my powers are only used for good. Now, I have put a spell on the Wilding-Davies and the Warners. If you or anybody harms them you will die a horrible death in 28 days. You will be screaming in agony with intolerable pain."

We got in the car and drove off. I told Terry that I was impressed with his talk. He laughed and said when he first came to Zimbabwe the Africans were scared of him. He finally figured out that they thought he was a tikoloshe. He said he was delighted to find a beneficial use for his handicap.

18

When Graham boarded his flight to Zimbabwe, the stewardess offered him a newspaper. He selected that day's *Telegraph* and was horrified to see Allan on the front page, covered in blood. Graham was shocked. He hadn't realized that things had got so bad.

After landing in Harare, he went to the minister of local government. This man had been minister of Higher Education when Graham ran the University and Graham had got along well with him. Graham thought this would be a good place to start and get insight into what was happening politically.

Graham waited to see the minister. After a couple of hours, the minister walked by. He refused to see Graham and was very offhanded. He said his deputy would see Graham. This was quite a snub to Graham. The deputy minister was the former District Administer for Chipinge. He had won the seat in the parliamentary elections for ZANU-PF and as a reward was given the post of deputy minister. His big help in securing the election for ZANU-PF was Joseph Chiminya. Joseph, as head of the CIO for Chipinge, was responsible for organizing electoral fraud, voter intimidation, and the beating and elimination of MDC party members.

The deputy minister sat down with Graham. He was carrying a large dossier. He pulled out a huge file on me. It contained letters I had written saying I wanted to overthrow the government, that I was a big player in the opposition. He said they had proof that our farm was used for opposition rallies. He said my house contained MDC literature and Roy Bennett held secret meetings with me. All of this was a complete fabrication.

When Joseph was in our house in June, he went through all our papers. There was nothing incriminating since I was not involved in politics. I think they must have got hold of my signature and fabricated these letters. What they genuinely found were the lyrics to Tracey Chapman's "Talking About A Revolution." Our band had been working on the song. They claimed the words were revolutionary writing of mine! They certainly had done a good job framing me.

There was nothing Graham could do. Graham could go as high as Mugabe if he wanted, but if Mugabe was shown this file it would be all over. We discussed what to do. Graham said the best he could do was to buy some time and peace for us and the Ashanti workers. He went back to see his old colleague, the former minister of Higher Education.

It was agreed that the Warners and myself would leave the country within thirty days. In return all of us would be left alone to pack up and leave in peace and none of our workers would be further victimized.

I drove back to Chipinge and had a meeting with our workers. Everyone was anxious and had put huge faith in Graham's ability to do something. Zimbabweans viewed him as a man of incredible ability. His stature in the country was huge.

When I explained that Graham had been unable to help us to return to Ashanti, a look of despair came over the faces of everyone present. We were still able to farm on Sweet Acres and also had a small section of coffee on Pete Human's farm. I told them that anyone who wanted to stay on, we could keep them employed. However, the

Ashanti workers feared that they would be victimized for confronting Joseph and the CIO. We arranged money for them and at night started moving them off by tractor and trailer to where they wanted to go. Our belongings were stacked on the lawn at the neighbouring Sweet Acres farm. Amy had already left for Canada.

I should have been angry, but I was numb. I should have been angry at being illegally robbed of my home, my business, my hopes and my dreams.

I should have been sad. Sad to see a beautiful productive enterprise destined to ruin. Sad to see hundreds of families left with no future.

I should have felt guilt; guilt from the failure to protect our workers, guilt for dragging Amy and my family through such an ordeal.

I should have felt despair. Despair in knowing that what is right and good had not prevailed. Despair that justice does not prevail.

I should have been comforted as our workers came to thank me for the good times, in knowing that we had made a positive impact on them.

Instead I felt nothing. I was numb from the shock.

We sold our cattle to a local tea estate. Even though they were dairy cattle, the tea estate slaughtered and sold the meat in their farm stores. We found homes for the horses and dogs. We tried our best to get jobs for any of our workers who wanted to move on. A moving truck came to move our belongings. They were packed in a container and started the long journey back to Canada.

My last night I sat on the lawn at Sweet Acres and looked over in the direction of Ashanti. The sun began to set and a line of darkness started to march across the valley and up the hill known as Excalibur. I could see a flock of parrots flying in to roost in the large mahogany tree in the Ashanti yard. They circled around and sensing something different, flew on to find another place to roost. There was no drumming from the farm villages. Darkness came silently.

The next morning I followed the moving truck out of Chipinge, down into the lowveld and onto Harare and Canada.

Five years later we were sitting with one of the few farmers in the district. He briefed us on what had happened after we left.

Within the next couple of months of our vacating Ashanti most of the farmers in our area were forced off their farms. Danmore ended up in South Africa. Although he has to work as an illegal immigrant and start at the bottom, he feels he is in an environment where his education and intelligence will get him ahead. He follows Zimbabwe politics and hopes for the day when people like him are appreciated and needed to rebuild the country.

Jason went back to his rural home and Lynette. The savings that he had carefully deposited in the Post Office Savings Bank over fifty years, became valueless thanks to Zimbabwe's astronomical inflation. His daughters are finding it hard to find husbands with the means to pay lobola for a traditional marriage. Jason and Lynette could not even buy corn seed and fertilizer to plant their annual crop. Zimbabwe had totally run out of foreign exchange and no longer grew seed corn or manufactured sufficient fertilizer. Jason was forced to buy a ZANU-PF membership card to get on the District Administer's list to receive United Nations food aid.

Samson, our old security guard, found it harder and harder to get fuel to run his pickup truck and keep his taxi service going. He hired a nephew to stay in the hut he had built on the occupied commercial farm. He had long given up trying to farm anything but found the benefits of being a "new farmer" still worthwhile. He was able to get some of the fuel that the government handed out to party supporters to buy their loyalty. He became further indebted to ZANU-PF to keep his business going and family fed. He felt that he could not refuse when they asked him to assist the wovits in carrying out violence on MDC supporters.

Tim lost his farm shortly after we lost ours. A high-ranking army officer arrived with his soldiers and let Tim remove nothing from his house or his farm. The army officer sold half a million dollars of coffee that Tim had bagged ready for export. The army officer was hailed as proof that the "new farmers" could produce large crops. However, the following year no coffee was sold.

Tim's youngest daughter was listening to one of her black school friends tell her about her new home. It was their new weekend home. She described the house and what was to be her new bedroom. Shock came over Tim's daughter when the girl described in detail, right down to the pictures on the walls, what had been her own room.

Tim is currently living in Harare waiting for the day when there is a return to the rule of law and recognition of property rights. He hopes to return to farming.

Pete Human and his father, descendents of the pioneers who made their way to this land from South African generations ago, found a note on their gate telling them to leave. They packed up and left.

Roy Bennett's popularity amongst the people of Zimbabwe continued to grow along with Mugabe's fear and hatred of him. Mugabe had him jailed and tortured. Roy fled to South Africa and was granted asylum. He later returned to Zimbabwe with assurances for his safety to participate in the government of national unity. Mugabe had him arrested again but was forced to free him after thousands of Roy's supporters surrounded the police station where he was being held. His supporters were afraid that the police would try to move him at night and kill him. His popularity is so large that people ask him if he would run for president. Zimbabwe is ready for a white president but not the rest of the world.

Allan and Aletta moved back to South Africa but have not given up hope of living in a peaceful and democratic Zimbabwe.

Joseph Chiminya went on to murder another two people. Since the murders were committed to help Mugabe and ZANU-PF stay in power he has never been arrested and taken to trial.

Many years later we decided we would drive and have a look at what had happened to Ashanti. As we left our friend's house and headed down the Eastern Border Road a tropical downpour started and the road began to swim in my vision...

CPSIA information can be obtained
at www.ICGtesting.com
Printed in the USA
LVOW04s0950030116

468283LV00008BA/37/P

9 781927 506417